M000268379

Beauty
from
ASHES

**AN INTENSIVE HEALING GUIDE
THROUGH THE BOOK OF NEHEMIAH**

By: Jessica Bretl

ISBN 978-1-0980-3824-3 (paperback)
ISBN 978-1-0980-3825-0 (digital)

Copyright © 2020 by Jessica Bretl

All rights reserved. No part of this publication may be reproduced, distributed, or transmitted in any form or by any means, including photocopying, recording, or other electronic or mechanical methods without the prior written permission of the publisher. For permission requests, solicit the publisher via the address below.

Christian Faith Publishing, Inc.
832 Park Avenue
Meadville, PA 16335
www.christianfaithpublishing.com

Printed in the United States of America

CONTENTS ....

ACKNOWLEDGMENTS

A special thank you to Sandy, without you this book would not have ever come to fruition. Your belief in me and God's calling is what kept spurring me on to take each step toward completion.

To every dear friend who has supported and upheld us these last six years, I wish I could name each one of you! Words cannot express how pivotal your presence and longsuffering support has been. My children and I are rebuilding and thriving directly because of your actively loving us like Jesus.

There are also several supporters who offered insight, gave of their time for preliminary editing, supplied me with a laptop, and used their gifts of design to make this all come together. This study truly is the work of so many of you and ultimately brought about by God.

Thank you.

INTRODUCTION ···

Beginning with the very theme behind this study's title, would you please set your focus on the verse below.

"To bestow on them a crown of *beauty instead of ashes*" (Isaiah 61:3, emphasis added).

"Beauty from ashes," that sounds like a quaint little phrase, doesn't it? In our current cultural trend of stenciled home decor, it is even likely to be displayed on many a rustic board or throw pillow. Do not get me wrong, I am enthralled by the craze of Cricut cutters and barn board signs. But this phrase, **beauty from ashes**? Well, it is more likely to stir mixed feelings. Those three words can easily evoke searing pain if in fact your life has been branded by them.

You see, in order for there to be beauty from ashes, there must first be ASHES. As in what was once WHOLE, standing as one thing, has been engulfed in fiery flames long enough and hot enough to reduce it to powdery ash.

A remnant of what was.

For those who sit amidst the ashes know that it carries an ache too despairing to simply be a casual quote. If you are holding this book, that means you may know a little something about the ruins of life. And you may be longing to know if there can ever be somehow, someway **beauty** from the most horrible pain you have barely survived. Dear one, there is.

The term "beauty from ashes" may not be specified in the book of Nehemiah, but it perfectly displays the heart of our God, who loves to bring beauty up from the most unlikely places. There is nothing too broken, too dirty, or too hard for Him. He formed man from the shapeless dust of the ground. He conquered sin and death on the cross for you. Surely, He can bend down over the charred remains of your life and, with His nail-scarred hands, mold lifeless heaps of ash into something beautiful.

In this study, we will read how God came to restore His people sitting amongst the ruins and rubble of their lives. We will learn by the example of those who have walked before us how to rebuild and stand against opposition. Get ready to see new beginnings and believe that there can, in fact, be beauty from your very own ashes. Let's pray.

For the eyes of the one reading these very words…Lord, would You reveal Yourself. Help them to see You on the pages of scripture and in their own lives. Teach them where and how to rebuild up from the specific ruins they face. To the heart that has been broken by pain…Father, tend to those dead places and breathe life into them. Use this time mightily, God, that Your name may be made great. AMEN!

Up from the Ashes ....

Be honest, how much do you know about the book of the Bible and the man named Nehemiah?

If right about now you are mentally scrambling and coming up empty, let me put you at ease. I have been right where you are. Until one day when God orchestrated a collision course involving His word and my life.

At the age of thirty, I was your typical stay-at-home Christian wife raising kids and keeping my home. We had a great church where we served in youth group, and I occasionally led a women's Bible study. It was preparing for one of these women's studies that led me to this book in the Bible called Nehemiah. We were teaching a marriage study, and I wanted to drive home the idea that as women, we are warriors for our marriages and families. I explored just enough to learn that Nehemiah called the people of Israel, God's Holy Nation, to stand and fight shoulder to shoulder on behalf of their sons, daughters, and families! *Perfect*, I thought, *this will demonstrate my "warrior" point quite nicely!* So the following week, I inserted that little verse into my teaching and *bam!* Nailed it! "Thank you, Nehemiah." Moving on, right? Well, not exactly.

From that little taste of Nehemiah, my curiosity had been peaked. Upon further reading, I realized I had not done the book justice by simply using it as a tiny reference piece. There were some powerful lessons in that book that I had missed. It begged some obvious questions. For instance, why did they NEED to stand shoulder to shoulder to defend their families in the first place?

For the first time, I began to devour scripture in a different way. I read line by line and began to fill my little yellow journal with notes. Here is what I began to really learn about Nehemiah…

God's chosen people, the Israelites, were attacked at the heart of their nation Jerusalem. The city walls were invaded and destroyed; their homes were ransacked and burned to the ground. Thousands of their people were carried off into captivity while their homeland smoldered behind them.

When I stopped to imagine what that must have been like, it was a heartbreaking scene, and I had all too casually used it as a cute little motivational speech. The book of Nehemiah picks up seventy years later when God calls him to go back to the rubble heaps of Jerusalem and lead the people to rebuild it. It was pretty powerful history!

I became so fascinated by this seemingly unknown book of scripture that it stirred a burning heart desire to share these lessons with other people! So in 2011, I attempted something I had never done before—to write up my own study notes.

You do not need to check your calendar to know it is now 2019. And yes, a logical question on your mind would be, "So what have you been doing with this material for all these years?" And after taking a deep breath, my answer would be…"I have been living it."

In the beginning of 2012, the walls of MY home were INVADED, and my entire life BURNED to the ground. Every square inch of my world felt RANSACKED and DESTROYED. I watched helplessly as those I love were taken captive. I lost my husband, my home, any sense of human security, my reputation, close relationships, an income, and the power to shield my children from any of it.

My entire world was ash. A dusty remnant of what was.

I stepped down from teaching Bible studies and stepped away from leading youth. Each day, I struggled to endure, and most days, I would have given anything NOT to have survived at all. On the outside, it may have seemed I was functioning pretty well, but on the inside, I was dying of despair in deep places I did not know existed. Nothing made any sense, and everything began to feel meaningless. I kept asking myself how I ended up here, but there were no answers. Engulfed in grief with no relief in sight, I began to lose my faith bearings.

So I wrestled with the Almighty.

I wrestled with God in ways I didn't think a good Christian should. Let me be frank so as to dispel any notion that I did well. Hear me—**I did not hold onto God. He held onto me**.

Year after painstaking year went by and all I could do was wander amidst the rubble to sift through the ashes for anything salvageable of my life. And even though I felt disconnected from the days of writing Nehemiah notes in my little yellow journal, God kept bringing the book of Nehemiah to my mind. So I thought maybe it would help if I could do something familiar like the old days of ministry and teaching.

I began plunking on my computer in an attempt to finally write study notes down. I would begin to see a real Bible study take form, but then I would face a day so full of despair, doubt, and agony that I would curl up and hide. In those moments, I concluded that I had NO business teaching anything. Besides, I didn't even know if I believed its message over my OWN life, let alone that I could share it with others.

I continued to wrestle with the Almighty.

I eventually came to a point where I could not deny God had given me instructions to teach Nehemiah, and that for me to do nothing would mean a willful disregard of His calling. I may have been bold enough to wrestle with Him, but I was not foolish enough to flat out defy Him. Even in my inner turmoil, I still WANTED to obey Him. I shared this conviction with a good friend of mine in order for her to hold me accountable. Suffice it to say that darling pest of a friend took her job seriously. She continually hounded me about the writing progress of the Nehemiah study. She even went as far as to put on HER calendar the day I agreed to officially start writing! That is what I call blessed persistence.

Surrendered to the Lord in a new way, I sat down to write THIS VERY introduction. And guess what? Something profound settled on me for the <u>very</u> <u>first</u> <u>time</u>!

Tears rolled down my face.

I found the old original yellow journal labeled "Nehemiah Notes" that I had started many years earlier. As I paged through its contents, I was struck by what should have been obvious to me all along, but I had not yet seen it. God gave me spiritual eyes to see for the first time the overwhelming parallel! Just as in the book of Nehemiah, the enemy broke through the walls of **MY** home to steal, enslave, and destroy. I watched the flames of sin engulf **MY** home as I stood helpless to put them out. I **TASTED** the shame of one of God's households falling and taking with it the name of Christ. All at once, I could **SEE** that the mess I had been living through was NOT a coincidence! The book of Nehemiah, that before I had only READ…now I had **LIVED**!

It was as if God was saying to me, "Okay, dear one, **NOW** you are ready to really teach this message." I had been branded by the Almighty, and now I clung to the desperate hope that it could be true for me, "beauty from ashes."

I sat for a while, holding my yellow notebook. I just kept running my hand over the words I had written long ago; I even envied my own handwriting. Oh, how I longed to melt into those pages and be transported back to that time—to be in my old life again. But deep down, I knew God had brought me too far to simply return unchanged. I was already a completely different person than the one who had taken those notes.

Trust me, loved one, when I confess that there were things that needed to be exposed to my own awareness. I was unknowingly growing prideful and self-righteous. My compassion for messy, non-sterile lives was waning. It was becoming all too easy to have all the right answers for other people. And my "put together" Christian life had unknowingly led me to inaccurate conclusions about the God of the universe.

I have learned so much from this long season of life that it was simply not possible to return to who I was. And now the details of Nehemiah are no longer obscure lessons of a small Old Testament book. I now feel them intensely. I am clinging to the VERY same God of Nehemiah to bring beauty from MY VERY OWN ashes. Do not miss this. The "beauty" from ashes part is that God may not change our circumstances, but He WILL change us.

So, dear one, that is how this study came to be, and now you are embarking on the rebuilding process of your own. You may have completely different ashes than mine, but God is able to rebuild any area of woundedness you are willing to rebuild with Him. Keep in mind that in the time it takes you to work through this book, you will not likely have fully restored circumstances. However, we will begin by meeting with Him to offer these piles of rubble in exchange for seeds of faith. And in time, beauty will rise.

So much growth can come from the rubble if we water it with Living Water.

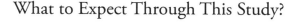

> So much growth can come from the rubble if we water it with Living Water.

What to Expect Through This Study?

Each lesson will begin by looking at the biblical text, which I have provided. We will explore the historical and biblical account to establish our foundation. I will offer some key points from the text but feel free to underline and make your own observations in the margins. We will then wrap up each lesson with a Personal Rebuilding section that will be very specific to you. While you may be eager for a quick "prescription pill" segment to ease the very immediate pain of your heart, it won't quite work that way. True healing takes time loved one, so try not to rush this process. Each lesson's personal rebuilding will build upon the next, so PLEASE commit to seeing it through until the very end.

I also included a song title at the end of each lesson. These are intensely personal songs God has sung over me as a healing balm, and I want to share them with you. Please take a few moments to play them for yourself, listening carefully to the lyrics, after each lesson before moving on.

Broken Walls

I strongly believe that we need a big picture understanding of Scripture before we can mine the depths of a particular book's details. Below you will find a very basic biblical timeline to help you place the historical story of Nehemiah. Glancing over it, note things you may recognize. Creation, Moses, and the time of the kings like King David. The Babylonian exile is when the Israelites were attacked and left in ruins. Locate the book of Nehemiah. This is the time period we are stepping into.

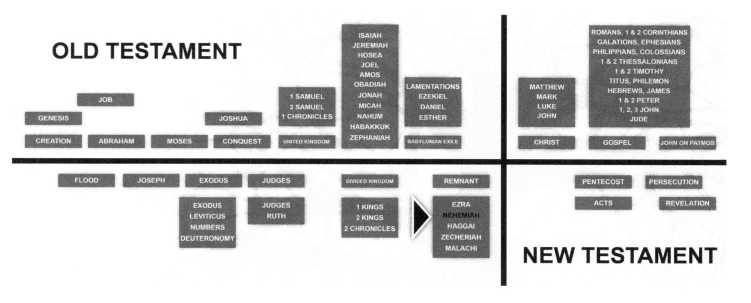

Let's set the stage and backdrop of our story.

In Bible times, the heart of a nation revolved around its central construct or city. The nation was defined by its strength and ability to protect itself and govern its own people. Walls were built around the cities, like that of Jerusalem, to fortify its rightful place in the land. To have weak and failing walls made you an easy target for an enemy. To have decimated walls suggested there had likely already been a battle that may have resulted in a change of power.

In the book of Nehemiah, we are entering a scene displaying just that. There had been two attacks by the rising superpowers of that time. Jerusalem's walls lay in ruin from the first invasion in 605 BC by the Babylonians, and then the second invasion in 586 BC by the Persians. This was a bigger deal than simply brick and mortar coming to ruin. The state of their walls and city brought disgrace and shame. The fall of a nation as a government was one thing, but these were God's chosen people! This was a people steeped in a unique historical heritage marked by miraculous provision from the Lord. They stood out time and time again to the nations around them as being defined by WHO THEIR GOD WAS. So how had this happened?

If we back up in Scripture, we read that both invasions on Jerusalem were allowed by God. The hearts of His people had strayed from Him, and so He used the powerful nations of Babylon and Persia to bring discipline to His wayward children. Their walls were destroyed, the Holy Temple was leveled, and many of God's people were carried away as slaves. It was a terrible time for the Israelite people, and it remained that way for seventy years.

When the time of discipline had come to an end, God began to bring the people out of captivity and reunite them. God first used Cyrus the Great, who ended the exile of the Israelites and gave them permission to return to Jerusalem. Historians agree there were several different waves of the Israelite's return. When we meet Nehemiah, some of the Israelites have already returned, and the new Persian king in power is King Artaxerxes I.

With the basics of history, we just learned we are finally ready to START the book of Nehemiah. There is so much growth ahead, and I am excited to walk it with you! Let's begin!

Go ahead and read chapter 1:1–4.

Nehemiah's Prayer for Jerusalem

1 The words of Nehemiah son of Hakaliah: In the month of Kislev in the twentieth year, while I was in the citadel of Susa, **2** Hanani, one of my brothers, came from Judah with some other men, and I questioned them about the Jewish remnant that had survived the exile, and also about Jerusalem. **3** They said to me, "Those who survived the exile and are back in the province are in great trouble and disgrace. The wall of Jerusalem is broken down, and its gates have been burned with fire." **4** When I heard these things, I sat down and wept. For some days I mourned and fasted and prayed before the God of heaven.

Key Points

- Nehemiah inquires about the remnant still in Jerusalem.
- He learns of the sad state Jerusalem and the people are in.

Reading it, did you notice words like *survived, exile, trouble, disgrace, broken, burned, wept, mourned*? Go back and underline them in the scripture text above.

Now try to place yourself in this moment with him. He just learned that those who had survived the attacks and exile are returning to the providence, but that the state of their homeland is quite dismal. They are in great trouble and disgrace.

What was his response in verse four? _____

He sat down and wept. For days, he mourned, fasted, and prayed. Scripture only says he mourned "some days," but I wish they had been a little more specific. Was it five days? Thirty days? While we do not know exactly how long he sat in mourning and fasting, it begs the question, how long have YOU been in mourning? Maybe you find yourself on day ONE of the hardest season of grief, not too far from *the moment everything changed.* Or maybe you have been sitting for YEARS, stuck in grief, unable to move. Please know that some things do require a good length of time to fully grieve. Do not be afraid to give yourself that time. However, there is another place we can find ourselves in the grieving process. Sometimes we move on from the wreckage and function pretty well on a daily basis. That is, until we stumble upon a picture, a person, or song, and in an instant, we are emotionally transported backward. Sights, smells, and sounds are powerful triggers that stimulate a connection from the external world to our inner being. It was no different for Nehemiah in his day. He was going about life as usual. He did not live in close proximity to Jerusalem to be affected on a daily basis, but it was the visit from his brother with news of home that grieved him to the core.

There are a hundred different places on the spectrum of pain and healing that you may find yourself. Take a moment now in prayer and ask God to reveal where you are on the grief spectrum. Place an X where you are currently and write how long you have been there. Make any other notes to signify where you have been in the grief process. Take as much time as you need. There is no right or wrong here. Honestly access where you will be starting from with the Lord. Also use this space to write any particular triggers, acknowledging them will ready you for future encounters.

PAIN & HEALING

PARALYZED BY PAIN	STILL EXCRUCIATING	MORE BAD DAYS	EVENLY GOOD AND BAD	MORE GOOD DAYS	MOVING ON WITH LIFE

No one wants to stay STUCK in grief unable to move on with their life. We all know that at some point, there needs to be forward motion. Nehemiah knew as much, and that is why it is a book about REBUILDING. And as with any rebuilding project, there comes that very first critical step.

Please peek at Nehemiah 1:5 and look only at the first three words of verse 5.

"Then I said: 'Lord, the God of heaven, the great and awesome God, who keeps his covenant of love with those who love him and keep his commandments.'"

Write them down _____ _____ _____ .

Did you hear that? It is a pretty small word—THEN. It may seem insignificant, but he had a THEN moment. He was in mourning and fasting, and THEN he turned to action. Regardless of how long the brokenness has had you in turmoil, maybe it is time for a THEN moment for you. Oh, how I pray the Lord may be stirring in you this very thing! Nehemiah turned his face toward the GOD of heaven and began to pour out his heart in confession and petition. You will have a chance to do this in your Personal Rebuilding section coming up, but for now, let's read his heart before God.

Read his prayer 1:5–11.

5 Then I said: "Lord, the God of heaven, the great and awesome God, who keeps his covenant of love with those who love him and keep his commandments, **6** let your ear be attentive and your eyes open to hear the prayer your servant is praying before you day and night for your servants, the people of Israel. I confess the sins we Israelites, including myself and my father's family, have committed against you. **7** We have acted very wickedly toward you. We have not obeyed the commands, decrees and laws you gave your servant Moses. **8** "Remember the instruction you gave your servant Moses, saying, 'If you are unfaithful, I will scatter you among the nations, **9** but if you return to me and obey my commands, then even if your exiled people are at the farthest horizon, I will gather them from there and bring them to the place I have chosen as a dwelling for my Name.' **10** "They are your servants and your people, whom you redeemed by your great strength and your mighty hand. **11** Lord, let your ear be attentive to the prayer of this your servant and to the prayer of your servants who delight in revering your name. Give your servant success today by granting him favor in the presence of this man." I was cupbearer to the king.

He turned to God and began to pray in very specific ways. It is one of the most powerful prayers I have ever read. Pay close attention to all that he does.

Key Points

- He acknowledges. First, he regards God as God.
- He asks to be heard. He is petitioning the Father for His ear.
- He confesses not only his own sin but the sin of the entire nation!
- He recounts their history with Him.
- He recalls the promises. God is faithful!
- He asks again to be heard, seeking an audience with God.
- He asks for actual requests and specifically names the provisions he will need.

> "
> The entire book of Nehemiah compels us to ACTION. We must model after scripture and rise up to do battle on behalf of what is broken and needs rebuilding in our own lives.
> "

Notice again he was getting up from his knees to ACT. He was not content to remain broken and grieved. He felt there was something to be DONE. The entire book of Nehemiah compels us to ACTION. We must model after scripture and rise up to do battle on behalf of what is broken and needs rebuilding in our own lives.

Below is another THEN verse. Circle the word *then* and underline the action the people took after it. Double underline what God's response was.

"Then they cried to the Lord in their trouble, and he saved them from their distress. He brought them out of darkness, the utter darkness, and broke away their chains" (Psalm 107:13–14).

It is time for you to rise up to act. There is work to be done, loved one. Prepare your heart as you to go into the time of personal rebuilding, asking God to stir the belief in you that beauty will rise.

Personal Rebuilding

In your personal reflection time today, you are going to name the pieces of brokenness in your own life. Do any of the words used in verses 1 to 4 describe how you once felt or feel now? What has left you feeling ransacked? What have you barely survived and still feel the lingering devastation of? Where have you felt exiled from? What disgraces have you walked, some that were maybe even self-inflicted? What relationship strain, job loss, or health issue has left your walls feeling burned to ashes?

Think about the words you would use to describe your situation, whether borrowed from the text of Nehemiah or your own. Invite God to bring the name of your specific areas of wounding. Use the space below to jot down those words on the stones of rubble. <u>Don't rush too quickly through this step. Fill every inch, if need be, as you pour it out before the Lord on paper.</u>

I am certain this process has the potential to be excruciating for some. Do not feel alone in whatever you may have just written above. I have cried tears upon tears over brokenness of my own, and I would not ask you to open the places you have bled from if I didn't believe God would be there. You are not alone; God will draw near to you. Sit and wait for Him. Ask HIM to replace all the wounds with a stirred HOPE that HE WILL bring restoration.

This next step will be important and will launch all of our rebuilding from here on out in this study. I am going to ask you to **<u>write</u> <u>out</u>** your own version of Nehemiah's prayer. TAKE YOUR TIME, LOVED ONE.

ACKNOWLEDGE. Start by acknowledging who God is. What do you know of Him? What has He done in your life? What are other names you know Him by?

_____

_____

_____

_____

_____

ASK TO BE HEARD. In your own words, ask Him to hear you and your heart.

_____

_____

_____

_____

_____

CONFESS. Share anything you feel prompted to confess before the Lord. If you are unsure, ask Him and sit in silence for a while to see if anything surfaces. Notice Nehemiah confessed sins on behalf of all the Israelites, as well as his father's household. If it is appropriate, carefully consider if there are family patterns or areas of sin that need to be acknowledged and confessed on behalf of your family line.

_____

_____

_____

_____

_____

RECALL HIS PROMISES. What are some things you know God has promised specifically that apply to your situation? Be patient here and try to be as specific as you can. Need some help? Here are a few verses to read that show promises He has made to us.

"He will give us rest" (Matthew 11:28–92).
"He will give us a new heart and spirit" (Ezekiel 36:26–27).
"He will work all things for good" (Romans 8:28).
"He will forgive and purity our sin" (1 John 1:9).
"He will fight for us" (Exodus 14:14).
"He will strengthen, help, and uphold us" (Isaiah 41:10).
"He will instruct, teach, and counsel us" (Psalms 32:8).
"He will encamp around us and deliver us" (Psalms 34:7).

On the next, page write out the promises you have in Christ.

HIS PROMISES:

_____
_____
_____
_____
_____

ASK AGAIN TO BE HEARD. God didn't miss it the first time, I assure you, but describe in different words this time your desperate need to be heard by Him.

_____
_____
_____
_____
_____

MAKE ACTUAL REQUESTS. What are some very tangible or literal requests you have regarding what you need to rebuild. Seek the Lord in prayer, listen for His leading. Remember your circumstances are specific to YOU, so be specific even if it seems trivial. For example, the sale of a home to be able start fresh, the courage to make a phone call, scholarship money for your child to go to camp, an accountability partner, forgiving someone or asking for forgiveness.

Look what James has to say regarding our prayers before our Heavenly Father,

"You have not because you ask not" (James 4:2).

Be bold in your literal requests to rebuild. God may not deliver them all on your preferred time line, but we know we have a God who hears us.

_____
_____
_____
_____
_____

God wants to give you practical tools to rebuild. He is not a genie in a bottle granting wishes, but He will bring tangible provisions to help you rise up from the ashes for His own Glory. **Now take a few moments and pray each of those sections you just wrote out as one continuous prayer to God.**

As we wrap up this first lesson, I know there is potential for wounds to be reopened and cause pain as you work through this study. However, I want to assure you…

"For the word of God is alive and active. Sharper than any double-edged sword, it penetrates even to dividing soul and spirit, joints and marrow; it judges the thoughts and attitudes of the heart" (Hebrews 4:12).

His Word is meant to be active and sharp. Blades of metal can pierce, but they can also be used as surgical tools. What the enemy intends to be a deathblow by a dagger can become a lifesaving surgical scalpel when given over to the hand of our God, the Great Physician. If God allows a piercing of your heart, He alone can tend to that place for its healing. Allow God to do the work He desires through this process.

Please find a version of the song below, including lyrics, to listen to on your phone or computer. Let it be a sweet time, set apart for God to breathe hope into your heart.

 "Beauty Will Rise" by Steven Curtis Chapman

Boldness and Banded Efforts

Hallelujah! You are still here! I am encouraged that you are trudging through the hard stuff to reach the beautiful parts. Let's keep digging in, shall we? Look back on page 16 at the very last sentence of Nehemiah 1 to remind yourself of Nehemiah's job position in the Citadel of Susa.

"Lord, let your ear be attentive to the prayer of this your servant and to the prayer of your servants who delight in revering your name. Give your servant success today by granting him favor in the presence of this man." I was cupbearer to the king."

He was ⸻⸻⸻⸻⸻⸻⸻⸻ to King Artaxerxes.

That meant he worked in close proximity with the king to provide him with drink. Nehemiah had undoubtedly been sovereignly placed there by God. Even so, you need to know in that time it was risky business being in the presence of a king. The book of the Bible right after Nehemiah is Esther, and even as the queen she feared instant death upon entering the king's court without being summoned. At this time in history, the whim of the king ruled, and Nehemiah knew enough to be very afraid.

Now read Nehemiah chapter 2:1–9. Then answer the following questions.

Nehemiah Sent to Jerusalem

2 1 In the month of Nisan in the twentieth year of King Artaxerxes, when wine was brought for him, I took the wine and gave it to the king. I had not been sad in his presence before, **2** so the king asked me, "Why does your face look so sad when you are not ill? This can be nothing but sadness of heart." I was very much afraid, **3** but I said to the king, "May the king live forever! Why should my face not look sad when the city where my ancestors are buried lies in ruins, and its gates have been destroyed by fire?" **4** The king said to me, "What is it you want?" Then I prayed to the God of heaven, **5** and I answered the king, "If it pleases the king and if your servant has found favor in his sight, let him send me to the city in Judah where my ancestors are buried so that I can rebuild it." **6** Then the king, with the queen sitting beside him, asked me, "How long will your journey take, and when will you get back?" It pleased the king to send me; so I set a time. **7** I also said to him, "If it pleases the king, may I have letters to the governors of Trans-Euphrates, so that they will provide me safe-conduct until I arrive in Judah? **8** And may I have a letter to Asaph, keeper of the royal park, so he will give me timber to make beams for the gates of the citadel by the temple and for the city wall and for the residence I will occupy?" And because the gracious hand of my God was on me, the king granted my requests. **9** So I went to the governors of Trans-Euphrates and gave them the king's letters. The king had also sent army officers and cavalry with me.

Key Points

- The king notices heaviness of heart in Nehemiah.
- Nehemiah is given a divine opportunity to ask for the king's aid.
- Nehemiah lists what he would need to help Jerusalem rebuild.
- The king grants all of his requests.

Pay close attention to a few powerful details.

What two emotions does Nehemiah feel in verses 1–2?

_____ and _____

What does he stop to do before answering the king specifically in verse 4?

_____

What three things does Nehemiah ask the king for in verses 4–8?

_____ _____ _____

Nehemiah is amazing! If there were an "I love Jerusalem" T-shirt, he would have be sportin' it. His love for his homeland and his trust in God is so evident! He turned to God in prayer BEFORE answering the king's question and then simply asked for exactly what he needed. I can just hear it… "Well most powerful king in the world, I would like you to let me leave, provide me with protection, and all the supplies and funds for the rebuilding venture of the entire Jewish people!" Wow, that is some boldness! And look closely. What does he attribute his success to at the end of verse 8? Underline it in your text above.

Nehemiah KNEW he had been granted favor by the sovereign hand of God Almighty! He had very real reason to fear the earthly king he was approaching and still he made bold requests. He trusted God for the courage and the success needed.

When you come to your Heavenly Father, are you fully aware of just how welcome you are? Take a moment to recognize how different it is for us to go into the throne room of OUR King; we are welcomed to come without fear! God is not just any king; He is also a good and loving Father.

Let's continue in our scripture passage to see WHY we need to boldly ask God for the things we need.

10 "When Sanballat the Horonite and Tobiah the Ammonite official heard about this, they were very much disturbed that someone had come to promote the welfare of the Israelites."

Key Points

- Sanballat and Tobiah are leaders in the surrounding area
- They are upset that someone is helping the Israelites

That's right! We already see opposition. You need to know opposition will come for you as well and almost immediately. The enemy, Satan, embodies destruction, division, and desolation. Any attempt on your part to restore, renew, or rebuild from his handiwork will be met with any and all attempts to keep you in ashes.

As we move on to the next portion of Scripture, it will be helpful to have a map of the walls around Jerusalem.

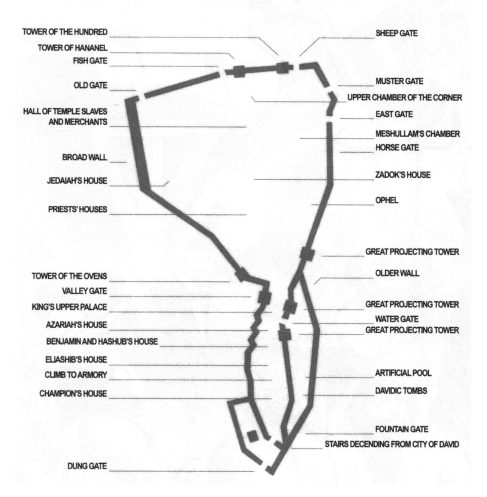

JERUSALEM'S WALL
IN NEHEMIAH'S DAY

TOWER OF THE HUNDRED

TOWER OF HANANEL

FISH GATE

OLD GATE

HALL OF TEMPLE SLAVES AND MERCHANTS

BROAD WALL

JEDAIAH'S HOUSE

PRIESTS' HOUSES

TOWER OF THE OVENS

VALLEY GATE

KING'S UPPER PALACE

AZARIAH'S HOUSE

BENJAMIN AND HASHUB'S HOUSE

ELIASHIB'S HOUSE

CLIMB TO ARMORY

CHAMPION'S HOUSE

DUNG GATE

SHEEP GATE

MUSTER GATE

UPPER CHAMBER OF THE CORNER

EAST GATE

MESHULLAM'S CHAMBER

HORSE GATE

ZADOK'S HOUSE

OPHEL

GREAT PROJECTING TOWER

OLDER WALL

GREAT PROJECTING TOWER

WATER GATE

GREAT PROJECTING TOWER

ARTIFICIAL POOL

DAVIDIC TOMBS

FOUNTAIN GATE

STAIRS DECENDING FROM CITY OF DAVID

Let's pick up in chapter 2:11–20.

Nehemiah Encourages the People to Rebuild the Walls

11 I went to Jerusalem, and after staying there three days **12** I set out during the night with a few others. I had not told anyone what my God had put in my heart to do for Jerusalem. There were no mounts with me except the one I was riding on. **13** By night I went out through the Valley Gate toward the Jackal[1] Well and the Dung Gate, examining the walls of Jerusalem, which had been broken down, and its gates, which had been destroyed by fire. **14** Then I moved on toward the Fountain Gate and the King's Pool, but there was not enough room for my mount to get through; **15** so I went up the valley by night, examining the wall. Finally, I turned back and reentered through the Valley Gate. **16** The officials did not know where I had gone or what I was doing, because as yet I had said nothing to the Jews or the priests or nobles or officials or any others who would be doing the work. **17** Then I said to them, "You see the trouble we are in: Jerusalem lies in ruins, and its gates have been burned with fire. Come, let us rebuild the wall of Jerusalem, and we will no longer be in disgrace." **18** I also told them about the gracious hand of my God on me and what the king had said to me. They replied, "Let us start rebuilding." So they began this good work. **19** But when Sanballat the Horonite, Tobiah the Ammonite official and Geshem the Arab heard about it, they mocked and ridiculed us. "What is this you are doing?" they asked. "Are you rebelling against the king?" **20** I answered them by saying, "The God of heaven will give us success. We his servants will start rebuilding, but as for you, you have no share in Jerusalem or any claim or historic right to it."

Key Points

- Nehemiah takes some time to fully assess the damage. (Just as you did by labeling your rubble heap.)
- Then he confidently casts the vision to the people.
- He shares with them how God called him.
- He shared that the favor of God granted him the support of the king to rebuild Jerusalem.

Great news! The people respond positively, and they were anxious to begin rebuilding right away! The less than great news, however, is that they immediately encountered more opposition. Do not miss the fact that the opposition has grown. At first, on the scene, we had met two men, Sanballat and Tobiah. Now they have added Geshem to their number. Opposition was not only increasing in number but also in intensity. The men opposing them had gone from simply being disturbed to outwardly mocking and ridiculing the Jews!

Look back at our text. Notice Nehemiah's response in verse 20. Who does Nehemiah claim will grant them success? _____ .

He knows who his God is and what He is capable of. He knows with God the success has already been awarded. Oh, how I long to develop such trust in my God!

Let's read on. Read all of chapter 3.

The Sections Assigned for Repair

3 1 Eliashib the high priest and his fellow priests went to work and rebuilt the Sheep Gate. They dedicated it and set its doors in place, building as far as the Tower of the Hundred, which they dedicated, and as far as the Tower of Hananel. **2** The men of Jericho built the adjoining section, and Zakkur son of Imri built next to them. **3** The Fish Gate was rebuilt by the sons of Hassenaah. They laid its beams and put its doors and bolts and bars in place. **4** Meremoth son of Uriah, the son of Hakkoz, repaired the next section. Next to him Meshullam son of Berekiah, the son of Meshezabel, made repairs, and next to him Zadok son of Baana also made repairs. **5** The next section was repaired by the men of Tekoa, but their nobles would not put their shoulders to the work under their supervisors.[1] **6** The Jeshanah[2] Gate was repaired by Joiada son of Paseah and Meshullam son of Besodeiah. They laid its beams and put its doors with their bolts and bars in place. **7** Next to them, repairs were made by men from Gibeon and Mizpah-Melatiah of Gibeon and Jadon of Meronoth-places under the authority of the governor of Trans-Euphrates. **8** Uzziel son of Harhaiah, one of the goldsmiths, repaired the next section; and Hananiah, one of the perfume-makers, made repairs next to that. They restored Jerusalem as far as the Broad Wall. **9** Rephaiah son of Hur, ruler of a half-district of Jerusalem, repaired the next section. **10** Adjoining this, Jedaiah son of Harumaph made repairs opposite his house, and Hattush son of Hashabneiah made repairs next to him. **11** Malkijah son of Harim and Hasshub son of Pahath-Moab repaired another section and the Tower of the Ovens. **12** Shallum son of Hallohesh, ruler of a half-district of Jerusalem, repaired the next section with the help of his daughters. **13** The Valley Gate was repaired by Hanun and the residents of Zanoah. They rebuilt it and put its doors with their bolts and bars in place. They also repaired a thousand cubits[3] of the wall as far as the Dung Gate. **14** The Dung Gate was repaired by Malkijah son of Rekab, ruler of the district of Beth Hakkerem. He rebuilt it and put its doors with their bolts and bars in place. **15** The Fountain Gate was repaired by Shallun son of Kol-Hozeh, ruler of the district of Mizpah. He rebuilt it, roofing it over and putting its doors and bolts and bars in place. He also repaired the wall of the Pool of Siloam, [4] by the King's Garden, as far as the steps going down from the City of David. **16** Beyond him, Nehemiah son of Azbuk, ruler of a half-district of Beth Zur, made repairs up to a point opposite the tombs[5] of David, as far as the artificial pool and the House of the Heroes. **17** Next to him, the repairs were made by the Levites under Rehum son of Bani. Beside him, Hashabiah, ruler of half the district of Keilah, carried out repairs for his district. **18** Next to him, the repairs were made by their fellow Levites under Binnui[6] son of Henadad, ruler of the other half-district of Keilah. **19** Next to him, Ezer son of Jeshua, ruler of Mizpah, repaired another section, from a point facing the ascent to the armory as far as the angle of the wall. **20** Next to him, Baruch son of Zabbai zealously repaired another section, from the angle to the entrance of the house of Eliashib the high priest. **21** Next to him, Meremoth son of Uriah, the son of Hakkoz, repaired another section, from the entrance of Eliashib's house to the end of it. **22** The repairs next to him were made by the priests from the surrounding region. **23** Beyond them, Benjamin and Hasshub made repairs in front of their house; and next to them, Azariah son of Maaseiah, the son of Ananiah, made repairs beside his house. **24** Next to him, Binnui son of Henadad repaired another section, from Azariah's house to the angle and the corner, **25** and Palal son of Uzai worked opposite the angle and the tower projecting from the upper palace near the court of the guard. Next to him,

Pedaiah son of Parosh **26** and the temple servants living on the hill of Ophel made repairs up to a point opposite the Water Gate toward the east and the projecting tower. **27** Next to them, the men of Tekoa repaired another section, from the great projecting tower to the wall of Ophel. **28** Above the Horse Gate, the priests made repairs, each in front of his own house. **29** Next to them, Zadok son of Immer made repairs opposite his house. Next to him, Shemaiah son of Shekaniah, the guard at the East Gate, made repairs. **30** Next to him, Hananiah son of Shelemiah, and Hanun, the sixth son of Zalaph, repaired another section. Next to them, Meshullam son of Berekiah made repairs opposite his living quarters. **31** Next to him, Malkijah, one of the goldsmiths, made repairs as far as the house of the temple servants and the merchants, opposite the Inspection Gate, and as far as the room above the corner; **32** and between the room above the corner and the Sheep Gate the goldsmiths and merchants made repairs.

True confession, I am mildly fascinated with the Amish community. Not so much the attire but the community—the way they do life together. The chapter we just read reminds me of a good ol' fashioned Amish barn raisin', where a whole town comes together to get one job done. I just love it! It makes me want to be a part of something meaningful like what we just read in Nehemiah.

If you are visual like me, go back to the text and highlight each of these references in a different color pencil. I used blue for all the WHO, green for the WHERE, and yellow for the HOW. It truly brought the page to life for me! Look at this compilation of all that is happening in this chapter…

WHO—Priests, sons, goldsmiths, perfume-makers, rulers, dads with the help of their daughters. Now you find some above. Circle any description of who is doing the work.

HOW—dedicated, laid beams, together with their families and neighbors in proximity to their homes, Baruch "zealously repaired." Again, find some on your own above and star other descriptions of how they are working.

WHERE—gates, sections, adjoining, walls, opposite his house, in front of their house.

I cannot help but be stirred inside. Picture what this must have been like! Can you imagine this from an aerial view? Imagine what it may have looked like to God! His people were working together side by side, doing hard work for the reputation of their name as God's people. And Baruch? I long to be described like he was! I want my tombstone to read: Jessica worked zealously for the Lord!

I have to pause here a second. My heart is gripped by this moment, and I do not want to let it slip away too quickly. Tears are filling my eyes over the longing I feel to live a life worthy of such a title. Lord God, let it be! Stir in each of us such determination to be your servants in this life. Give us the heart of Baruch for your Glory.

I have met a few "Baruchs" over the last seven years. God has brought some of THE most amazing servants of Christ to minister to me in my darkest days. At the end of a long hard day, I would pull out a small Post-it Note pad from my nightstand and jot down names and notes to remember their kindness. They are the WHOs of my story. They stood with me and my kids as the side-by-side team, I could not have survived without. Would you please allow me to share some of those notes with you in hopes it would bless you to see the body of Christ at work?

They emptied my gutters, brought me coffee, made meals, and let me cry on their couches. These are just some of the workers who stood shoulder to shoulder with me, and I will never be able to thank them sincerely enough.

Ahem…well, I guess I took a deeper trip down memory lane than I intended. Let's see if I can bring this back to where we left off.

We were looking at the WHOs of the story, but I also want to look at the HOW. I want us to marvel at the brilliance of how strategic they were in having each family build directly in front of where their homes would be. This allowed for easy access; it saved time and brought personal motivation in making sure the craftsmanship was sound. They built side by side, spanning their efforts widely around the city perimeter. It was an organized and well-thought-out system. Nehemiah had truly been gifted by the Lord to orchestrate such a crucial task. However, there were other benefits to positioning the workers the way he did, and we will look at that in the next section. For now, I feel like it is time for you process through how some of this applies to your rebuilding efforts.

Personal Rebuilding

Remember Nehemiah showed great bravery in approaching the earthly king, Artaxerxes. Look up Hebrews 4:14–16. What does it say about how we can approach the KING OF KINGS?

_____

Looking back on your first assignment, what emotions do you feel as you approach our King about the words written on that page of rubble?

_____

Now look back to the prayer you wrote on page 19. What two "requests" are the most important as you prepare to rebuild some of the broken areas in your life? How can you take a step toward making them happen?

_____

_____

We touched on the opposition that will surely come against your desire for restoration. Satan wants to keep you in his ashy playground. Without allowing it to turn to fear, what are some things, people, or circumstances that you anticipate the enemy may use to stand in your way? How can you prepare for them?

_____

_____

_____

_____

_____

Like Nehemiah, let us recall with confidence He who has the power to bring victory to our lives. Stand firm, dear one, in God's calling over you to rebuild. His power is greater than any enemy against you.

Lastly for today, I want you to spend some time considering the WHO, HOW, and WHERE of your own story. I don't know about you, but I would have missed so many neat things happening in Nehemiah chapter 3 if we hadn't taken the time to break down each of those areas. Take a moment to pray and think over your life so far before answering the following questions.

Who are your WHOs? Whose names come to mind as having come alongside you? How have they shown up on your behalf?

_____

_____

_____

_____

_____

WHERE is your rebuilding happening? More than likely it is a combination of both a literal location and a personal/spiritual level. (Examples in your own walk with Him, a marriage, financially, parenting, a new job, an addiction, etc.)

_____

_____

_____

_____

_____

HOW would you describe your effort in the rebuilding process? Are you working diligently with all your heart like Baruch? Are you dedicating small advancements along the way to God like this Jews did?

_____

_____

_____

_____

_____

Father God, I pray over the details shared above. Please continue to stir their heart toward the hope of what you can bring. Hold back the opposition and bring wave after wave of encouragement and newness into their life. AMEN.

Oh please, don't give up, loved one. Please come back to where you left off and continue. There are some really neat things ahead, and I would hate for you to quit now. I'll be here waiting. Don't forget to take some time to worship through this next song.

 "The Sun is Rising" by Britt Nicole

LESSON 3

Up from the Ashes

Yes! You made it! And just in time for probably my favorite chapter in the entire story, Chapter 4. Read 4:1–3.

The Workmen Guard against the Adversaries

4 1 When Sanballat heard that we were rebuilding the wall, he became angry and was greatly incensed. He ridiculed the Jews, **2** and in the presence of his associates and the army of Samaria, he said, "What are those feeble Jews doing? Will they restore their wall? Will they offer sacrifices? Will they finish in a day? Can they bring the stones back to life from those heaps of rubble-burned as they are?" **3** Tobiah the Ammonite, who was at his side, said, "What they are building-even a fox climbing up on it would break down their wall of stones!"

Key Points

- News of the rebuilding is spreading.
- Sanballat is angry and incensed.
- Their enemies are publically ridiculing them. "Can they bring the stones back to life from those heaps of rubble, burned as they are?"

THIS IS SO AMAZING I could do a cartwheel! (If, in fact, I knew how to do a cartwheel.) The symbolism here is very moving but incredibly bold. Hang with me here.

In the verses you just read, Sanballat painted a bleak scene of utter hopelessness. The rubble, burned stones, and charred remains are all ultimately describing death. I did some digging and discovered the word he is using here is "revive." Sanballat was mocking the possibility of *reviving* anything from those heaps of ash. Oh, but he did not know the very One who breathes life into all things!

Please read Ezekiel 37, the Valley of Dry Bones, as I burst with anticipation for you!

The Valley of Dry Bones

37 1 The hand of the Lord was on me, and he brought me out by the Spirit of the Lord and set me in the middle of a valley; it was full of bones. **2** He led me back and forth among them, and I saw a great many bones on the floor of the valley, bones that were very dry. **3** He asked me,

"Son of man, can these bones live?" I said, "Sovereign Lord, you alone know." **4** Then he said to me, "Prophesy to these bones and say to them, 'Dry bones, hear the word of the Lord! **5** This is what the Sovereign Lord says to these bones: I will make breath[1] enter you, and you will come to life. **6** I will attach tendons to you and make flesh come upon you and cover you with skin; I will put breath in you, and you will come to life. Then you will know that I am the Lord.' "**7** So I prophesied as I was commanded. And as I was prophesying, there was a noise, a rattling sound, and the bones came together, bone to bone. **8** I looked, and tendons and flesh appeared on them and skin covered them, but there was no breath in them. **9** Then he said to me, "Prophesy to the breath; prophesy, son of man, and say to it, 'This is what the Sovereign Lord says: Come, breath, from the four winds and breathe into these slain, that they may live.'" **10** So I prophesied as he commanded me, and breath entered them; they came to life and stood up on their feet-a vast army. **11** Then he said to me: "Son of man, these bones are the people of Israel. They say, 'Our bones are dried up and our hope is gone; we are cut off.' **12** Therefore prophesy and say to them: 'This is what the Sovereign Lordsays: My people, I am going to open your graves and bring you up from them; I will bring you back to the land of Israel. **13** Then you, my people, will know that I am the Lord, when I open your graves and bring you up from them. **14** I will put my Spirit in you and you will live, and I will settle you in your own land. Then you will know that I the Lord have spoken, and I have done it, declares the Lord.'"

This is not just a powerful word; it is the EXACT SAME WORD—REVIVE.

To "revive" does not just mean to make something come to life. It is more about what was once alive, meeting the finality of death, then coming BACK to life once again!

It shouts of the miraculous, the impossibility outside of an ALL-POWERFUL God's intervention! Look back specifically at the taunting words of Sanballat at the end of Nehemiah 4:2. Write them down.

"Can they bring these stones _____ , burned as they are?"

It is as if God answers his mockery by doing EXACTLY that. You see, there is strong belief and archeological evidence to suggest the Jews did not just clear away all of the rubble to start over. They rummaged through the remains to pull up OUT OF THE ASHES, some of the SAME burned stones to REBUILD WITH THEM!

I am sure the Israelites could have found all new stones, BUT I love that by reviving some of the old stones, the scoffer is made a fool. It is no accident that it is the same word; God used it to pour the mockery of Sanballat back onto his very own head. Hear this, loved one, God will not be mocked.

"The Valley of Dry Bones" could not be a more powerful depiction of God being the author and giver of the breath of life. In the very same way that God restored dry dead bones (by giving them flesh, tendons, and breath), God was at work to restore the lifeblood of Jerusalem. He was breathing life back into what had been dead for over seventy years! I think we need an "AMEN!"

So what does all of this mean for you and me? Allow me to make some safe assumptions. While the Israelites reused some of the stones, not all of them were used. Some of the rubble needed to be cleared out of the area as they were no longer strong enough to be foundational. Likewise, we need to access our own rubble—what needs to be fully cleared away and what needs to be pulled up from under the ash—and reset as foundation stones. Whether it is a clean slate, a renewal of what was or a combination of both, God is breathing LIFE into something that was dead.

Beauty from ashes, my dear one, is a precious and glorious thing. Underline the words of hope in the following verses that most speak to your heart.

> And provide for those who grieve in Zion—to bestow on them a crown of beauty instead of ashes, the oil of joy instead of mourning, and a garment of praise instead of a spirit of despair. They will be called oaks of righteousness, a planting of the Lord for the display of his splendor. They will rebuild the ancient ruins and restore the places long devastated; they will renew the ruined cities that have been devastated for generations. (Isaiah 61:3–4)

Let's read three more verses before we wrap up this lesson. Read Nehemiah 4:4–6.

4 Hear us, our God, for we are despised. Turn their insults back on their own heads. Give them over as plunder in a land of captivity. **5** Do not cover up their guilt or blot out their sins from your sight, for they have thrown insults in the face of the builders. **6** So we rebuilt the wall till all of it reached half its height, for the people worked with all their heart.

Key Points

- Nehemiah prays for God to defend them by turning the insults back on their own head.
- They returned to building the wall.

How does it describe their work at the end of verse 6?

"For the people _____ with all their _____ ."

It doesn't say all their strength, but all their HEART! They were passionate about this project, and the result was progress. Nehemiah's wall was beginning to take shape! Praise the Lord. Now let us take some time to focus on the progress of your own rebuilding as well.

Personal Rebuilding

Be very sure of one thing, friend, Satan is not just going to sit by and watch you become restored! You NEED to be aware the enemy will try to derail your progress. What has the enemy already done to mock you? How would "Sanballat" describe your situation?

_____

_____

_____

_____

_____

Nehemiah's first response to the mockery was to go to God in prayer. He left vengeance in its rightful place, but at the same time, he asked God to intervene on their behalf. Write out a prayer for God to intervene on your behalf regarding the specifics you shared above.

_____

_____

_____

_____

_____

We are a few lessons in, and this rebuilding process may already be feeling wearisome. Where is your hope level that God can breathe life into your valley of dry bones? Be honest, if you are struggling to believe it, that is okay. On the next page mark where you are on the hope spectrum provided. Pour it out in prayer before the Lord.

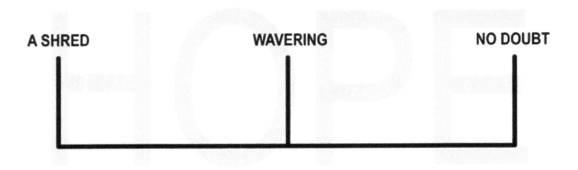

| A SHRED | WAVERING | NO DOUBT |

Hope seen in others can be an inspiring thing! My daughter was only eight years old at the time her dad left. Oh, how that little girl longed for her daddy to return and for life to go back to the way it was. We prayed together many times for that to happen. One night, after tucking her into bed, I thought I heard music. So I got up from the couch and crept down the hallway to investigate. I was not prepared for what I overheard outside her bedroom door. My little girl was crying and singing in her sweet little voice, "Greater things are yet to come…greater things are still to be done **in my home…home…home**." I went to my knees and began to sob quietly. While my anger burned at the injustice of his betrayal, my spirit beamed with pride at the hope and faith of this precious girl. Faith like a child is a beautiful thing; it believes and hopes with abandon! Wherever you are on the spectrum of hope and despair, rally, dear one. God sees you!

Remember there are two kinds of rubble, some to be removed entirely and some to be reestablished. Take some time to separate out the words used in your <u>original</u> rubble heap or new words God brings to mind, write them in the diagram below.

RUBBLE TO
REMOVE

Examples of things to clear away—gossip, suicidal thoughts, toxic people, addiction, sexual sin, people pleasing, etc.

Take a moment to look at the words you just wrote on those stones. Consider carefully just how crucial it is that you have a fresh start by removing them. Letting go of them can be really challenging, especially if it is from a person or substance addiction. If anything you listed above is abuse or sin, you cannot walk this part alone. Get yourself an accountability partner, counselor, or meet with a pastor to seek godly help.

Do not take this step lightly precious one. If the Lord is prompting you here, do not turn away but instead press in. Make a plan for success, get radical by deleting Facebook, ending an ungodly relationship, switching jobs, or moving, if need be. Whatever you need to be free and start again, please write it on the stones and commit to removing them.

I know a man who is in the process of hauling large stumbling blocks from his life as I write this. He is going to great lengths to set himself up for success in obeying God. That has meant he remove himself from a community of people that led him into sin, including the virtual community of Facebook. He chose to leave his apartment, although still paying rent there, to accept a free room elsewhere. When he recognized his propensity to feel weak in times of loneliness, he made arrangements to safeguarding himself in those times. He is surrounding himself with men who will hold him accountable and is working to make right the wrongs he has committed over the years. Basically, he is willing to go to ANY length necessary to reach a strong foundation in which to build up from. It is remarkable and rare to see such conviction followed by action! It reminds me of a definition of biblical perseverance I once read. It said, "Perseverance is a long slow obedience in the same direction." The man I described is walking with that level of commitment and perseverance, and so should we.

> "Perseverance is a long slow obedience in the same direction."

Lord, I commit to removing all of these things from my life. Please show me how and bring others to come along side me as I do the work of clearing these things from my life.
I am committed to removing (read the things listed on the rubble above).
Help me, Father. Amen.

Now we need to list all of the stones that need to be reused from the <u>original</u> rubble heap you wrote and any that God may bring to your mind now. Take some time to pray and write on the diagram provided.

RUBBLE TO REUSE

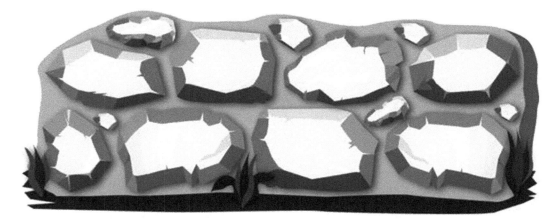

Examples to reuse—identity in Christ, your marriage, ministry, substance abuse program, forgiveness, etc.

I ask you to consider the importance, no matter how big or small, of each stone you list above. What will you need to help bring victory? Write those things on the stones as well and consider finding one friend to share them with.

Searching out reusable stones is a beautiful pursuit. Keep in mind, however, that just because it is the right thing, does not make it the easy thing. I have a dear friend who displays this more beautifully than I could imagine, so permit me to share about her a bit.

When my life fell apart, she was one of the people who rushed in to help. I had never met her before, but she knew a thing or two about sitting in ashes herself. Three years prior, her home had also faced the fiery heat and tasted the smoke of inferno. She had heard through a mutual friend that my husband had left his family. So this amazing, introverted beauty stepped out of her comfort zone and asked me to dinner. We sat across a table at a local food place, total strangers, but with a surprisingly instant bond! I will never forget one of the first things she said. "I am so sorry that you have anything in common with me." Familiar pain filled her eyes, and I knew exactly what she meant—she hated the horrible thing that now bonded us.

But *from that night on, we were like peas and carrots*! Ha! Forgive the random splash of humor, but I had to lighten it up a bit! We hung out quite a bit after that night. We went shopping, did house projects, started a single-parent ministry, and our kids became friends. OH, and we talked and talked and texted and talked some more. We cried, prayed, and vented countless hours together. Basically we wore a path between our two rubble heaps in order to help each other sift through ashes and begin to rebuild.

That was seven years ago. My whole point in sharing all about this godly friend of mine is this: Over the last year or so, God has begun to do some unexpected miracles in her story! Her ex-husband, who had left her and their son, has slowly been returning to the Lord! God is transforming him into a new man, and with that, he is returning to his family after eight long years! I have truly never seen anything like it!

My sweet friend had a choice to make. God was dusting off a huge foundational stone in her life labeled "covenant," and He was offering it back to her. Not many people get that kind of opportunity, and even less would be called to do such a thing. But this friend felt specifically called by God to reestablish that particular piece from her rubble heap. These two imperfect human beings are choosing the VERY HARD WORK of restoring their covenant. They are not under any pretense that it will be easy! They are very aware that this is a miracle, not to be confused with a fairy tale. Satan is already bringing all sorts of circumstances to thwart God's plan for beauty from eight years of ashes. I feel utterly privileged to watch this Bible-sized miracle unfold before my very eyes. I cannot help but notice countless signs of new life growing up around them. There are signs of growth not only for themselves but for their son, extended family, and even friends. Those of us close enough to witness the rebuilding of their home feel the backsplash of its blessings! Praise the Lord!

I share that testimony with my friend's permission to say that it will not always be easy to reestablish foundational stones. So pray intently for God's specific leading in the stones He may be calling you to reestablish for the base you will build upon.

Let's pray. Lord, I commit to reestablish (<u>read</u> <u>off</u> <u>each</u> <u>thing</u> <u>listed</u> <u>above</u>) as a new foundation in which to build the rest of my life. Help me to see these stones as vital to obeying your call on my life. Bring me the tools I need to place them where they belong and keep them there. AMEN.

You are doing well, loved one. Keep working with all your heart. You will begin to see progress. Soak in today's song before you go on with your day.

 "Come Alive" by Lauren Daigle

LESSON 4 ....

Remember, Our God Will Fight for Us

Welcome back! Up until now, we have been inching our way through the book of Nehemiah. I promise we are about to pick up speed and cover more ground. The last four lessons ahead may get a bit bumpy, but there is really exciting stuff ahead too, so hang on tight.

Let's start with bumpy stuff! Watch how the schemes of the enemy begin to intensify and unfold in interesting ways. Please read Nehemiah 4:7–9.

> **7** But when Sanballat, Tobiah, the Arabs, the Ammonites and the people of Ashdod heard that the repairs to Jerusalem's walls had gone ahead and that the gaps were being closed, they were very angry. **8** They all plotted together to come and fight against Jerusalem and stir up trouble against it. **9** But we prayed to our God and posted a guard day and night to meet this threat.

Key Points

- Opposition continues to grow. We are no longer talking about just a few men. Three whole separate groups of men have joined Sanballat and Tobiah.
- They are growing in their anger as they see the Israelites making progress.
- It is no longer just mocking words; they plot to fight and stir up trouble.
- Nehemiah's powerful response is "BUT we prayed to our God."
- Practical steps are taken by posting a guard day and night to keep watch.

Isn't it interesting that the enemy has a way of stirring others to join him and increase the pressure to deter us from doing exactly what God has called us to. Nehemiah is scarcely affected and simply makes a plan to be on guard. There is so much I can learn from Nehemiah as he continually turns to the Lord first in times of trouble.

Now read Nehemiah 4:10–13.

> **10** Meanwhile, the people in Judah said, "The strength of the laborers is giving out, and there is so much rubble that we cannot rebuild the wall." **11** Also our enemies said, "Before they know it or see us, we will be right there among them and will kill them and put an end to the work." **12** Then the Jews who lived near them came and told us ten times over, "Wherever you turn, they will attack us." **13** Therefore I stationed some of the people behind the lowest points of the wall at the exposed places, posting them by families, with their swords, spears and bows.

Key Points

- The workers are growing tired and weary. They are losing momentum.
- They are reciting the words of their enemy and fearing their intent toward them.
- Neighboring Israelites come to recite and inflate the rumors, stirring even greater fear.
- Nehemiah positions armed men along the vulnerable places of the wall for protection.

Here are a few key things we should take away from these verses for our own battles. When we are physically drained, we also are less able to stand our ground, and we lose momentum. Also, when we hear negative words spoken over us, we need to take them captive immediately and replace them with the truth. Otherwise, when we repeat them to ourselves, we begin to believe them as well. And lastly, when the enemy ramps up his attack against us, we need to ramp up our armor in response to him and stand prepared to fight.

Now here comes the most popular verse of Nehemiah (the one I stumbled upon all those years ago), and they are powerful words that surely warrant their popularity. Please read Nehemiah 4:14.

> After I looked things over, I stood up and said to the nobles, the officials and the rest of the people, "Don't be afraid of them. Remember the Lord, who is great and awesome, and fight for your families, your sons and your daughters, your wives and your homes."

Key Points

- Nehemiah stops and takes a minute to "look things over."
- Nehemiah stands up to rally and encourage the people!
- He emboldens them not to be afraid, but instead…
- "REMEMBER the LORD who is great and awesome!"
- Nehemiah calls his people to "fight for your families."

The word *remember* is all over scripture! God knows our tendency to forget His faithfulness and how desperately we need to remember His hand in our lives. Here is a brief overview of just a few biblical examples.

Genesis 9:15–16. The rainbow was a **reminder** that God promised he would never again flood the earth.

Deuteronomy 16:1–3. The Passover was to **remember** God's deliverance from Egypt.

Numbers 15:39. The tassels on their garments were a **reminder** of God's commands.

Deuteronomy 32:7. The older generations were instructed to **recount** the stories of God. They were to **remind** the young ones of all God had done.

Joshua 4:7. Stones were taken from the middle of the Jordan and set up on the other side to serve as a **memorial.** So they would **remember** God opening the Jordan so they could walk through on dry ground.

The book of Nehemiah alone has the word *remember* in it ten times! Nehemiah knows recalling God's provisions from THEN will empower the people to trust Him NOW. These are exiles returned home for the sake of their God and their families. Now is the time for them to rise. Now is the time to stand shoulder to shoulder with one another. Now is the time to fight for their brothers, sons, daughters, wives, and homes!

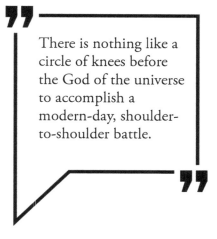

There is nothing like a circle of knees before the God of the universe to accomplish a modern-day, shoulder-to-shoulder battle.

When my home was under siege, there were plenty of moments people prayed with me, for me, and over me. However, one night in particular remains engrained as a shoulder to shoulder fight for my family. My pastor and his wife, new friends, and their spouses, long-standing friends and spouses, and I all met together. All fourteen of us circled up in a living room to do spiritual battle on behalf of my home. It was a truly powerful and humbling experience. Those loved ones took turns addressing our Heavenly Father on behalf of my husband, children, and home. With their arms wrapped around my shoulders, we pounded the doors of heaven and God's ears with heartfelt pleas for His intervention. It was abundantly productive, even though it did not alter my circumstances immediately. Two things happened that night; it reoriented my hope back on to my GOD, and it refueled my mind, body, and spirit to continue on! There is nothing like a circle of knees before the God of the universe to accomplish a modern-day, shoulder-to-shoulder battle. I am eternally grateful for them.

Let's pick up in verse 15 to find out what God did. Read verse 15.

15 "When our enemies heard that we were aware of their plot and that God had frustrated it, we all returned to the wall, each to our own work."

Key Points

- Their enemies learned that Nehemiah knew of their plot.
- "Because GOD had frustrated their work"
- They returned to their work.

How amazing is that? Their enemies abandoned their plans to physically attack the workers of the wall because they knew they had lost the element of surprise. Not only that but they knew exactly who was responsible for ruining their plans.

One more time, who does it say frustrated the enemies work? _____

More than likely, no one is threatening you physically or verbally as you work through this book. We live in a different culture and time that seems safe enough from such attacks. Oh, but we still have an enemy in our day. Sometimes it is easy to tell when the enemy is pressing in, but other times, he flies under our radar, so we do not accurately perceive who is behind the struggle. God and His heavenly forces are real, but just as real are Satan and his armies. We cannot pretend otherwise. In our lives, we have an invisible battle raging against us and around us.

"For though we live in the world, we do not wage war as the world does. The weapons we fight with are not the weapons of the world. On the contrary, they have divine power to demolish strongholds" (2 Corinthians 10:3–4).

In this verse above, underline the two things it says that do NOT apply to us. Then circle what we DO have. Let's pick up where we left off. Please read verse 16–20.

16 From that day on, half of my men did the work, while the other half were equipped with spears, shields, bows and armor. The officers posted themselves behind all the people of Judah **17** who were building the wall. Those who carried materials did their work with one hand and held a weapon in the other, **18** and each of the builders wore his sword at his side as he worked. But the man who sounded the trumpet stayed with me. **19** Then I said to the nobles, the officials and the rest of the people, "The work is extensive and spread out, and we are widely separated from each other along the wall. **20** Wherever you hear the sound of the trumpet, join us there. Our God will fight for us!"

Key Points

- Half the men worked, half stood guard.
- They carried materials to work with in one hand and a sword in the other.
- Nehemiah continues to access, oversee, anticipate, and strategize.
- He establishes the sound of a trumpet blast to signify an attack and a call for help.
- He finishes verse 20 with "Our God will fight for us."

The image of this moves me deeply. Can you picture it? They are working with one hand AND equipped for battle with the other. It is exactly how I want God to look down and see me living, doing everyday life for Him with one hand and carrying His Word as my sword in the other. Let it be Lord!

Nehemiah strategizes brilliantly for the people to defend themselves, BUT he knows GOD will ultimately be fighting the battle. It is amazing how God's involvement and power is never far from his mind. Read verses 21–23.

21 So we continued the work with half the men holding spears, from the first light of dawn till the stars came out. **22** At that time I also said to the people, "Have every man and his helper stay inside Jerusalem at night, so they can serve us as guards by night and as workers by day." **23** Neither I nor my brothers nor my men nor the guards with me took off our clothes; each had his weapon, even when he went for water.

Key Points

- From morning until night, they were vigilant; they did not even change clothes.
- They made practical steps to face practical needs. Safety and progress.

These men stood on high alert, and they were not going to give the enemy a single moment of vulnerability! How incredible is that! We may not need to stand guard for our safety, but we can be practical in our assessment of the challenges we face.

When my husband first left, one of the struggles I faced was a very practical one. I had postponed my career to be a stay-at-home mom for the previous eight years and, therefore, had no degree to earn a decent income for my kids. The jobs I would be considered for would barely cover daycare expenses, and my kids needed my presence now more than ever. I could feel the fear of the financial needs ahead rising up. I recited out loud the pleas of Psalms 143 so many times a day that I began to have it memorized.

> 1 LORD, hear my prayer, listen to my cry for mercy;
> in your faithfulness and righteousness come to my relief.
> 2 Do not bring your servant into judgment,
> for no one living is righteous before you.
> 3 The enemy pursues me, he crushes me to the ground;
> he makes me dwell in the darkness like those long dead.
> 4 So my spirit grows faint within me; my heart within me is dismayed.
> 5 I remember the days of long ago;
> I meditate on all your works and consider what your hands have done.
> 6 I spread out my hands to you; I thirst for you like a parched land.
> 7 Answer me quickly, LORD; my spirit fails.
> Do not hide your face from me or I will be like those who go down to the pit.
> 8 Let the morning bring me word of your unfailing love, for I have put my trust in you.
> Show me the way I should go, for to you I entrust my life.
> 9 Rescue me from my enemies, LORD, for I hide myself in you.
> 10 Teach me to do your will, for you are my God;
> may your good Spirit lead me on level ground.
> 11 For your name's sake, LORD, preserve my life;
> in your righteousness, bring me out of trouble.
> 12 In your unfailing love, silence my enemies; destroy all
> my foes, for I am your servant. (Psalms 143)

Eventually a very natural solution came. I like to clean; it clears my head; and I am good at it. So I started to take on home cleaning jobs. It was good money, very flexible, and allowed me the most amount of time with my kids. Seven years later, I am still cleaning most of those homes, and the families have actually become dear friends to me.

God answered my prayers to provide financially AND to be very present for the raising of my two little ones. As it turns out, however, God had more in mind than just meeting my practical financial needs. Over time, I began to realize another sweet and tender gift the Lord had been bestowing upon me through my job.

Let me first confess that scrubbing toilets was not necessarily my definition of a glamorous career, but I came to see that God was doing something special with that time. Upon arriving to a job, the first thing I would do was turn on Pandora to my Jason Gray station. I had hours each day alone, just me and my worship music.

Without fail, even when my heart was as hard as stone, God would begin to meet me in the darkest, ugliest, most painful places of my soul. When I could not open my Bible to feed myself truth, God in His tenderness sang it gently over me. First, I could hear it and then feel it…until eventually my heart of stone would break. Countless times in a client's home, I would be on my knees sobbing. There have been so many healing moments with Him over intimate lyrics from a worship song.

So sure, mopping someone else's floor had its humbling moments, but it was not just about giving me money to live, it gifted me with TIME to process and heal. Working as a bank teller or cashier would have put food on the table, but it wouldn't have allowed me uninterrupted time and space for Him to put my broken heart back together. I did not see what He was doing at the time, but I do now.

"Lord, if I have not said it recently, thank you for that."

The next section of Scripture takes a much-needed break from the wiles of Sanballat and Tobias. I know this has been a lengthy chapter, but hang in just a bit longer with me as we wrap up.

In Nehemiah 5, we see a break in the focus from the external battle to a particular struggle happening within their own community.

Read Nehemiah 5:1–13.

> **5 1** Now the men and their wives raised a great outcry against their fellow Jews. **2** Some were saying, "We and our sons and daughters are numerous; in order for us to eat and stay alive, we must get grain." **3** Others were saying, "We are mortgaging our fields, our vineyards and our homes to get grain during the famine." **4** Still others were saying, "We have had to borrow money to pay the king's tax on our fields and vineyards. **5** Although we are of the same flesh and blood as our fellow Jews and though our children are as good as theirs, yet we have to subject our sons and daughters to slavery. Some of our daughters have already been enslaved, but we are powerless, because our fields and our vineyards belong to others." **6** When I heard their outcry and these charges, I was very angry. **7** I pondered them in my mind and then accused the nobles and officials. I told them, "You are charging your own people interest!" So I called together a large meeting to deal with them **8** and said: "As far as possible, we have bought back our fellow Jews who were sold to the Gentiles. Now you are selling your own people, only for them to be sold back to us!" They kept quiet, because they could find nothing to say. **9** So I continued, "What you are doing is not right. Shouldn't you walk in the fear of our God to avoid the reproach of our Gentile enemies? **10** I and my brothers and my men are also lending the people money and grain. But let us stop charging interest! **11** Give back to them immediately their fields, vineyards, olive groves and houses, and also the interest you are charging them-one percent of the money, grain, new wine and olive oil." **12** "We will give it back," they said. "And we will not demand anything more from them. We will do as you say." Then I summoned the priests and made the nobles and officials take an oath to do what they had promised. **13** I also shook out the folds of my robe and said, "In this way may God shake out of their house and possessions anyone who does not keep this promise. So may such a person be shaken out and emptied!" At this the whole assembly said, "Amen," and praised the Lord. And the people did as they had promised.

Key Points

- Some of the people raised a complaint about the nobles.
- The nobles were operating like the godless cultures around them instead of like God's people.
- They were exacting usury, which is fancy talk for charging high interest rates.

- Nehemiah confronts them by making a compelling case for their people.
- The Israelite nobles were receptive! They repented of their sin and agreed to change this practice.
- Nehemiah calls for the priests to perform a ceremonial cleansing and a binding oath with these men.
- The people praised the Lord and did as they promised.

It is a rare and powerful thing to see people willing to hear the voice of truth and feel a sense of conviction. These men are a great example of having a teachable heart and acting on that conviction to make it right. Please read verses 14–19.

14 Moreover, from the twentieth year of King Artaxerxes, when I was appointed to be their governor in the land of Judah, until his thirty-second year-twelve years-neither I nor my brothers ate the food allotted to the governor. **15** But the earlier governors-those preceding me-placed a heavy burden on the people and took forty shekels[1] of silver from them in addition to food and wine. Their assistants also lorded it over the people. But out of reverence for God I did not act like that. **16** Instead, I devoted myself to the work on this wall. All my men were assembled there for the work; we[2] did not acquire any land. **17** Furthermore, a hundred and fifty Jews and officials ate at my table, as well as those who came to us from the surrounding nations. **18** Each day one ox, six choice sheep and some poultry were prepared for me, and every ten days an abundant supply of wine of all kinds. In spite of all this, I never demanded the food allotted to the governor, because the demands were heavy on these people. **19** Remember me with favor, my God, for all I have done for these people.

Key Points

- Nehemiah describes the way he conducted himself honorably as an overseer of the people.
- He and his men served the people and did not exploit their position of power.
- They gave to the people rather than taking from them like the previous rulers.
- He displayed characteristics of a true servant leader.

It sounds like Nehemiah is giving us a giant summary speech, doesn't it? Why is he reviewing all of this now? Well, there has been a great amount accomplished on the wall, and he can see completion ahead. Hopefully you can too! Take a small breather if you need it, but then head into your application time excited to keep rebuilding. DO NOT GIVE UP!

Personal Rebuilding

We are about halfway through this material, and your time spent here will not be in vain loved one. Do NOT discount the power of the work you are doing. Fight the voices that say this is futile as you work through these questions prayerfully.

Where is it that you are under attack the most? Is it depression and doubt? Are discouraging words being spoken over you? Maybe you are simply losing steam on finishing this very study?

Identify any and all tactics the enemy is using to thwart your progress.

_____

_____

_____

Fear took hold for the people of Israel when they began RECITING the words of their opposition. What negative words have been spoken over you that need to be silenced?

_____

_____

_____

Over EACH detail listed above, I ask that you pray the following prayer out loud. Take as long as you need.

My Father and Creator, You alone see me with utter clarity and love me still. I take these words said of me... _____ *and ask that You would replace them with the TRUTH. I cast out all fear and lies from the enemy in the name of Jesus. Amen.*

Now in big letters, write the word *lies* as many times as you need to cover them all up.

Nehemiah continually brought the people together to work, pray, and stand guard. Think of one or two people who you can ask to "post watch" for you in prayer, someone to be specifically praying over you and encouraging you. Write their name(s) here.

_____ & _____

We are told over and over in God's Word to REMEMBER! It is now time for you to REMEMBER His faithfulness specifically to you. List any and every way God has answered you, brought relief, helped or comforted you.

_____

_____

_____

_____

_____

Lastly today, say out loud as they did, "Our God will fight for us!" And He will. AMEN!

I know I say it every time, but our next lesson is truly the pinnacle of the story and my favorite part. There are jewels just ahead, please don't miss it. Please enjoy every word of this next song. Let it wash over you as a personal message from the Lord to you!

The next sheet provided is another option for your list to REMEMBER. If you are visual like me, it helps to lay it out on the timeline of your life. Don't forget to soak in some worship.

 "Even This Will Be Made Beautiful" by Jason Gray

TODAY

Use this page by turning it lengthwise to create a timeline of your life.

1. List the year you were born.
2. Think of the first time you remember hearing about or experiencing God. What is an icon you could use to symbolize it?
3. Write in any significant childhood experiences that shaped you (good or bad). Use a simple icon to represent that time.
4. Draw a cross on the timeline of when you accepted Christ as your Savior.
5. Write in any specific experiences that impacted your faith or you seeing God work in your life. Use simple pictures to represent them.
    • people who poured into you
    • prayers answered
    • churches you attended
    • verses or sermons that spoke change into your life
    • marriage, kids, deaths, jobs, etc.

   Symbol Suggestions: Cross for Christ, sun for good times, dark cloud for hard times, stick people, grave for the loss of a loved one, red cross for medical issues, green for growth, black for turmoil,

BORN

Many Faces of the Enemy

Rebuilding from painful ashes of your life is hard work. I have no doubt you have needed a break along the way or maybe even considered giving up. Dear one, there is a turning point just ahead! Whether you see it yet or not, the time you are spending here before the Lord has the potential to bring you into wholeness and healing from the most brutal of circumstances. Go with me into the next part of our scripture passage.

Read Nehemiah 6:1.

The Plots of the Adversaries

6 1 When word came to Sanballat, Tobiah, Geshem the Arab and the rest of our enemies that I had rebuilt the wall and not a gap was left in it-though up to that time I had not set the doors in the gates.

Key Points

- The wall is rebuilt with not a gap left in it, except for the gates.

Excuse me, what did he just say? After all of that, did he just nonchalantly mention that the wall itself is complete? He sure did! All that is left to do is drop the gate doors into place, and they are fully finished! Imagine the excitement that must be stirring for the workers of the wall! A turning point is ahead for them as it very well may be for you. By all means, let hope arise, but at the same time, let's not forget I did warn you that Sanballat and Tobiah would return. As they reenter the scene, pay close attention to the devious adjustments they have made in their approach to stop the Israelites.

Read verses 6:2–4.

2 Sanballat and Geshem sent me this message: "Come, let us meet together in one of the villages[1] on the plain of Ono." But they were scheming to harm me; **3** so I sent messengers to them with this reply: "I am carrying on a great project and cannot go down. Why should the work stop while I leave it and go down to you?" **4** Four times they sent me the same message, and each time I gave them the same answer.t

Key Points

- Sanballat and Tobiah have invited Nehemiah to a meeting.
- Nehemiah discerns that it is a trick to lure him out from behind the safety of the wall.
- He replies that he cannot leave the project.
- Four times, they ask him to meet them, and four times, Nehemiah gives the same answer.

Umm…okay! I know I have a weird sense of humor, but this part of the story is awkwardly hilariously to me! After taunting and threatening Nehemiah for weeks, these men are now asking Nehemiah to come out to "play!" And even more entertaining is Nehemiah's response that he is ready for this "busy." I find this thoroughly amusing! Clearly Sanballat and Tobiah are grasping at straws here, and that has a way of making people act a fool. Nehemiah simply declines their backyard invite and remains focused on the task before him.

Time and time again, Nehemiah displays an incredible amount of discernment, something we need to wisely take note of as the enemy schemes and plots over our rebuilding process. God alone provides such insight. We are told in the book of James that we can boldly ask to be given the wisdom we need.

> **"If any of you lacks wisdom, he should ask God, who gives generously to all without finding fault, and it will be given to him" (James 1:5).**

Lord, would you grant each of us the wisdom to see clearly.

While "ballat and the boys" failed miserably in their last attempt, it does not get better from here. Read verses 5–9.

> **5** Then, the fifth time, Sanballat sent his aide to me with the same message, and in his hand was an unsealed letter **6** in which was written: "It is reported among the nations-and Geshem[2] says it is true-that you and the Jews are plotting to revolt, and therefore you are building the wall. Moreover, according to these reports you are about to become their king **7** and have even appointed prophets to make this proclamation about you in Jerusalem: 'There is a king in Judah!' Now this report will get back to the king; so come, let us meet together." **8** I sent him this reply: "Nothing like what you are saying is happening; you are just making it up out of your head." **9** They were all trying to frighten us, thinking, "Their hands will get too weak for the work, and it will not be completed." But I prayed, "Now strengthen my hands."

Key Points

- Sanballat sends a sealed letter containing rumors that Nehemiah is looking to take up his own kingship.
- He urges Nehemiah to meet with him for his own protection from the wrath of King Artaxerxes.
- Nehemiah denies the claims, knowing they are fabricated.
- He rightly discerns the true motive behind the letter.
- He prayed God would strengthen his hands.

Oh, please tell me you are laughing! Sanballat has fabricated this elaborate rumor to frighten and trick Nehemiah into trusting him. Smells like desperation to me! Nehemiah plainly denies its validity and turns to God regarding a more pertinent mater. He prays for the literal strength he and all the workers need to push through muscle aches and fatigue; they need the physical strength to persevere.

I know I have chuckled over the last two efforts by the enemy to deceive Nehemiah, but be prepared. There will be nothing comical about their next evil design. It is about to take a heartbreaking turn in the verses ahead.

Read verses 10–14.

> **10** One day I went to the house of Shemaiah son of Delaiah, the son of Mehetabel, who was shut in at his home. He said, "Let us meet in the house of God, inside the temple, and let us close the temple doors, because men are coming to kill you-by night they are coming to kill you." **11** But I said, "Should a man like me run away? Or should someone like me go into the temple to save his life? I will not go!" **12** I realized that God had not sent him, but that he had prophesied against me because Tobiah and Sanballat had hired him. **13** He had been hired to intimidate me so that I would commit a sin by doing this, and then they would give me a bad name to discredit me. **14** Remember Tobiah and Sanballat, my God, because of what they have done; remember also the prophet Noadiah and how she and the rest of the prophets have been trying to intimidate me.

Key Points

- Shemaiah, a fellow Israelite, warns Nehemiah of a plot on his life. He even suggests that they meet in the safety of the sacred house of God.
- Nehemiah discerns that God had not sent Shemaiah.
- Shemaiah had been bribed by Tobiah and Sanballat.
- Nehemiah asks God not to forget this act, and other attempts to intimidate him by his enemies.

Sadly, I am not laughing anymore. My heart is weighted with sorrow over those last verses. One of Nehemiah's very own people, within the walls of Jerusalem, just betrayed him. Tell me, is there anything more excruciating than the betrayal of those closest to you?

> **If an enemy were insulting me, I could endure it; if a foe were raising himself against me, I could hide from him. But it is you, a man like myself, my companion, my close friend, with whom I once enjoyed sweet fellowship as we walked with the throng at the house of God. (Psalms 55:12–14)**

I have sobbed countless tears on those very pages in my Bible as it lay open before me. The intimacy and vulnerability of certain relationships make for the most horrific pain when they are betrayed or abandoned. And while I do not want this study to focus solely on the particular wound of divorce, I feel it worth spending a moment addressing. Please feel free to skip to the next page if divorce is not a part of your walls of ruin.

First, let me just say there are biblical grounds for divorce, where God allows for protection and freedom for those who fall within certain circumstances. What I am about to share is not meant to condemn those who have been divorced but explain the gravity of pain it brings.

Marriage is unique in the depths to which it exposes your heart, mind, body, and soul. It is a powerful human relationship that is designed to bring profound intimacy and spiritual union. Therefore, it poses great opportunity for deep soulful suffering. I have known abuse, betrayal, hurt from a parent and abandonment by a friend. I am acquainted with significant loss and heartache, including the miscarriage of my second baby.

Even so, I can say there is something starkly different regarding the agony of severing a marriage covenant. I firmly believe there is a biblical reason WHY divorce brings a distinctive soul tearing pain.

I have wrestled with the Lord over this in prayer time and time again, asking Him desperately why this is exponentially more excruciating than ANY other horrific pain, abuse, or loss I have ever endured. His gentle answer has continually been the same to me, that yes…it is different.

Marriage is the only earthly relationship stamped by God to resemble His Holy Trinity. God designed marriage to reflect the unity, submission, and faithful character the trinity embodies. When we enter into the covenant of marriage, God himself stands as an overseer of our marital vows. His word literally says "the two become one flesh," and because we are more than just our fleshly bodies, there is a joining of a spiritual component as well. There is something HAPPENING in the spiritual realm when we STAND at the altar and declare I DO. In order to divide two people fused on a spiritual level, it will be excruciating.

Lawyers and judges may divide the earthly accumulations of the two, but there is no amount of precision in which either soul walks away unmarred. It is like the forceful pulling, tearing, and snapping of tightly interwoven tendons and muscle fibers. That is the picture God kept bringing to my mind when I pleaded to understand why I still hurt in places I could not describe, even years after my husband left.

God has an intense and intentional purpose in His plan for marriage. When that is betrayed and the covenant abandoned, it goes against God's very design, and it destroys places in our souls we cannot see. That is why when Psalm 55 says, "If an enemy were insulting me, I could endure it," because when it is someone interwoven into us, it feels impossible to endure. With God, however, all wounds have the potential to be healed, even divorce. It is not impossible, just more complex. It may simply take a bit longer to separate out and hand over to our Great Physician. Understanding the unique nature of marriage will hopefully help in that process.

Clearly there are many different relationships with the power to wound.

Psalm 55:12–14 also says, "My companion, my close friend, with whom I once enjoyed sweet fellowship as we walked with the throng at the house of God." A parent, sibling, or friend can also be described as "sweet fellowship." And the loss of that relationship can tear you apart profoundly due to the depth in which you loved them. In Psalms 55, David is actually referring to his deep love for his friend, Jonathan. He and Jonathan had been like brothers to one another and cherished each other dearly. The unfortunate circumstances of Jonathan's father being King Saul and David being named by God as the rightful King, brought a unique set of challenges for the two friends. This world often brings unique challenges for all our different types of relationships as well.

I want to be very careful how I communicate this next part; I have no desire to be careless with my words. The semi-comparison I can make is that after my husband left me and the church, I experienced some unintentional but quite misguided distance by other people. It was as if my husband leaving me raised some suspicions for them about me as a wife and woman of God. This planted a LOT of self-doubt and conflict inside of me that went on to wage war against the very foundations of my faith. It was devastating to me and just as much a feeling of betrayal as my spouse leaving. I lacked the discernment then to measure what was true and what was not because of how dear they were to me. It took a long time for me to wade through what they intended to be accountability but, in truth, was mistakenly unhelpful. Now as I look back over those dynamics, I am able to stand firmly in the truth while offering them grace and still have a deep love for them.

Regardless of the exact nature of the relationship, to be hurt by one of our own, brings a wound that requires the power of God to fully heal. Do not let the infection of anger and un-forgiveness set in and spread; it will invade every area of your heart.

This has been a long hard lesson, dear one, and I may have opened some festering areas that need tending. Please take all the time you need with the Lord as you work through your personal rebuilding time.

Personal Rebuilding

Thinking back over your last four personal application sessions...

How has He provided what you said you needed to rebuild?

_____

_____

_____

What do you still have to follow through on?

_____

_____

_____

Who did you ask to stand shoulder to shoulder with you or be your prayer support?

_____

_____

_____

Are you obeying God with the clearing and reusing of your rubble?

_____

_____

_____

Some of our greatest rubble remains from wounds by "one of our own." Spend time jotting down only the initials of a person you feel caused that level of betrayal. Briefly bullet point any areas unresolved regarding those relationships.

_____

_____

_____

_____

_____

_____

_____

_____

Now this is the delicate part. Go back over that list and PRAY fervently over the details above for the supernatural power to forgive their actions and hand it over to God who judges justly. Humbly seek God's direction in any offense you may have committed and may need to seek forgiveness for.

Pray over the verses below and ask God for the supernatural strength to align your heart with His scripture.

"When they hurled their insults at him, he did not retaliate; when he suffered, he made no threats. Instead, He entrusted himself to him who judges justly" (1 Peter 2:23).

"It is mine to avenge; I will repay" (Deuteronomy 32:35a).

"Do Not Say, 'I'll pay you back for this wrong!' Wait for the LORD, and he will avenge you" (Proverbs 20:22).

"But to you who are listening I say: Love your enemies, do good to those who hate you, bless those who curse you, pray for those who mistreat you" (Luke 6:27–28).

This next worship song has brought me to my knees more times than I can count. Do not discount how impactful music can be to usher you into His presence for healing.

 "Nothing is Wasted" by Jason Gray

LESSON 6 ....

Completion

Completion. Take a moment to let that word settle into your being. The word *completion* is laden with emotion if we comprehend all of the blood, sweat, and tears it took to reach. Picture an exhausting load finally being able to be set down or an arduous journey coming to a glorious reprieve. It is like the lid being lifted off a prison pit so dark that you had almost forgotten what sunlight was. That is what the Israelites of Jerusalem are gazing at; completion.

Read Nehemiah 6:15–16.

> **15** So the wall was completed on the twenty-fifth of Elul, in fifty-two days. **16** When all our enemies heard about this, all the surrounding nations were afraid and lost their self-confidence, because they realized that this work had been done with the help of our God.

Key Points

- The wall was completed in fifty-two days.
- All of their enemies heard the news.
- The enemies were afraid and lost confidence because…
- Even THEY REALIZED the work had been done with the help of GOD!

Man! I really need to learn how to do a cartwheel! I am without proper outlet once again as I read these verses! Dear one, do we GET the magnitude of this? Even the audience of wicked oppressors KNEW God had helped them. When God chooses to display His unstoppable PLAN, even the stonehearted will ACKNOWLEDGE GOD AS SUPREME!

> **"As surely as I live, says the Lord, every knee will bow before me; every tongue will acknowledge God" (Romans 14:11).**

Those of us who have placed our faith in Jesus Christ bow willing, but those who refuse Him WILL BE MADE to bow the knee at His return. The enemy may scoff for a season, but one day, they will KNOW we stood faithful because our help came from God! Amen!

In Nehemiah's story, it was their enemies who had been keeping a close eye on them and their progress. For us, however, it is more likely that we have a different type of audience. Our kids, family members, coworkers, and friends all have a front row seat to the demonstration of our faith. Look around in this broken world, there is no shortage of hurting people. So when they see the hope we cling to despite our burdens, they will take notice! They will be watching to see who we turn to, how we behave, what comes out of our mouths, and whether or not we will still serve God in the midst of our pain.

Whether it is the individual who is in need of hope or an enemy who hopes to see you fail, those observing WILL ULTIMATLEY REALIZE the work in you has been done with the help of GOD, just like in Nehemiah's day!

Read verses 17–19.

17 Also, in those days the nobles of Judah were sending many letters to Tobiah, and replies from Tobiah kept coming to them. **18** For many in Judah were under oath to him, since he was son-in-law to Shekaniah son of Arah, and his son Jehohanan had married the daughter of Meshullam son of Berekiah. **19** Moreover, they kept reporting to me his good deeds and then telling him what I said. And Tobiah sent letters to intimidate me.

Key Points

- There are family ties to Tobiah and some of the nobles.
- Tobiah uses them for information through correspondence.
- Tobiah continues to try to intimidate Nehemiah.

This guy is relentless! Even though the wall has been completed, still he schemes for information. Nehemiah continues to pay him no mind, for he has greater things to prepare for.

The story is not over, and I absolutely love what is ahead! You do not want to miss it! I may even have an extra fun assignment for you in this chapter.

Continuing on please read all of chapter 7.

Nehemiah Appoints Rulers for Jerusalem

7 1 After the wall had been rebuilt and I had set the doors in place, the gatekeepers, the musicians and the Levites were appointed. **2** I put in charge of Jerusalem my brother Hanani, along with Hananiah the commander of the citadel, because he was a man of integrity and feared God more than most people do. **3** I said to them, "The gates of Jerusalem are not to be opened until the sun is hot. While the gatekeepers are still on duty, have them shut the doors and bar them. Also appoint residents of Jerusalem as guards, some at their posts and some near their own houses." **4** Now the city was large and spacious, but there were few people in it, and the houses had not yet been rebuilt.

The List of Returning Exiles

5 So my God put it into my heart to assemble the nobles, the officials and the common people for registration by families. I found the genealogical record of those who had been the first to return. This is what I found written there: **6** These are the people of the province who came up from the captivity of the exiles whom Nebuchadnezzar king of Babylon had taken captive (they returned to Jerusalem and Judah, each to his own town, **7** in company with Zerubbabel, Joshua, Nehemiah, Azariah, Raamiah, Nahamani, Mordecai, Bilshan, Mispereth, Bigvai, Nehum and Baanah): The list of the men of Israel: **8** the descendants of Parosh, 2,172 **9** of Shephatiah, 372 **10** of Arah, 652 **11** of Pahath-Moab (through the line of Jeshua and Joab), 2,818 **12** of Elam, 1,254 **13** of Zattu, 845 **14** of Zaccai, 760 **15** of Binnui, 648 **16** of Bebai, 628 **17** of Azgad, 2,322 **18** of Adonikam, 667 **19** of Bigvai, 2,067 **20** of Adin, 655 **21** of Ater (through Hezekiah), 98 **22** of Hashum, 328 **23** of Bezai, 324 **24** of Hariph, 112 **25** of Gibeon, 95 **26** the men of Bethlehem and Netophah, 188 **27** of Anathoth, 128 **28** of Beth Azmaveth, 42 **29** of Kiriath Jearim, Kephirah and Beeroth, 743 **30** of Ramah and Geba, 621 **31** of Micmash, 122 **32** of Bethel and Ai, 123 **33** of the other Nebo, 52 **34** of the other Elam, 1,254 **35** of Harim, 320 **36** of Jericho, 345 **37** of Lod, Hadid and Ono, 721 **38** of Senaah, 3,930 **39** The priests: **40** of Immer, 1,052 **41** of Pashhur, 1,247 **42** of Harim, 1,017 **43** The Levites: **44** The musicians: **45** The gatekeepers: **46** The temple servants: **47** Keros, Sia, Padon, **48** Lebana, Hagaba, Shalmai, **49** Hanan, Giddel, Gahar, **50** Reaiah, Rezin, Nekoda, **51** Gazzam, Uzza, Paseah, **52** Besai, Meunim, Nephusim, **53** Bakbuk, Hakupha, Harhur, **54** Bazluth, Mehida, Harsha, **55** Barkos, Sisera, Temah, **56** Neziah and Hatipha **57** The descendants of the servants of Solomon: **58** Jaala, Darkon, Giddel, **59** Shephatiah, Hattil, **60** The temple servants and the descendants of the servants of Solomon, 392 **61** The following came up from the towns of Tel Melah, Tel Harsha, Kerub, Addon and Immer, but they could not show that their families were descended from Israel: **62** the descendants of **63** And from among the priests: **64** These searched for their family records, but they could not find them and so were excluded from the priesthood as unclean. **65** The governor, therefore, ordered them not to eat any of the most sacred food until there should be a priest ministering with the Urim and Thummim. **66** The whole company numbered 42,360, **67** besides their 7,337 male and female slaves; and they also had 245 male and female singers. **68** There were 736 horses, 245 mules, [1] **69** 435 camels and 6,720 donkeys. **70** Some of the heads of the families contributed to the work. The governor gave to the treasury 1,000 darics[2] of gold, 50 bowls and 530 garments for priests. **71** Some of the heads of the families gave to the treasury for the work 20,000 darics[3] of gold and 2,200 minas[4] of silver. **72** The total given by the rest of the people was 20,000 darics of gold, 2,000 minas[5] of silver and 67 garments for priests. **73** The priests, the Levites, the gatekeepers, the musicians and the temple servants, along with certain of the people and the rest of the Israelites, settled in their own towns. When the seventh month came and the Israelites had settled in their towns.

Key Points

- Nehemiah establishes order by appointing positions and rules regarding the wall gates.
- He puts his brother Hanani in charge of all of Jerusalem.
- Hanani was a man of integrity and feared God more than most men did.
- "So my God put it into my heart." Nehemiah is confident of who is directing him.
- Reestablishing order, government structure, living arrangements, authenticating genealogy.

Now that the wall is complete, Nehemiah spent time organizing and setting up leaders to maintain a structured government for the people. Regarding how this applies to the rebuilding work in your life, you need to know that none of us will be fully complete this side of heaven. However, a particular season or lesson can reach completion. A season of ruins can come to restoration in our lives as it is about to for the people of Israel.

The nation of Israel is nothing if not ceremonial. They mark significant moments, dates, miracles, and lessons with meaningful rituals and monuments. All throughout the Old Testament, they are erecting pillars, altars, and rock piles all intended to remember the work of their God. This next chapter is a gripping demonstration of His chosen ones reinstating their heritage and coming full circle. It is truly a thing of beauty where there once were only ashes.

Please read chapter 8:1–6 while I get a box of tissues.

Ezra Reads the Law to the People

8 1 all the people came together as one in the square before the Water Gate. They told Ezra the teacher of the Law to bring out the Book of the Law of Moses, which the Lord had commanded for Israel. **2** So on the first day of the seventh month Ezra the priest brought the Law before the assembly, which was made up of men and women and all who were able to understand. **3** He read it aloud from daybreak till noon as he faced the square before the Water Gate in the presence of the men, women and others who could understand. And all the people listened attentively to the Book of the Law. **4** Ezra the teacher of the Law stood on a high wooden platform built for the occasion. Beside him on his right stood Mattithiah, Shema, Anaiah, Uriah, Hilkiah and Maaseiah; and on his left were Pedaiah, Mishael, Malkijah, Hashum, Hashbaddanah, Zechariah and Meshullam. **5** Ezra opened the book. All the people could see him because he was standing above them; and as he opened it, the people all stood up. **6** Ezra praised the Lord, the great God; and all the people lifted their hands and responded, "Amen! Amen!" Then they bowed down and worshiped the Lord with their faces to the ground.

Key Points

- All of the people assembled as one man, one unified group.
- A wooden stage had been built JUST for this very occasion. This was a significant turning point in their history.
- Ezra brings out the Law of Moses to be read out loud; God's law written for Israel.
- As Ezra opens the book, all of the people rise to their feet in honor of God's Word.
- They lifted their hands in praise and shout AMEN! Joyful to finally be restored.
- Then they bowed down in worship with their faces to the ground, acknowledging the sin that had led to the discipline of their nation in the first place.
- All the people listened attentively from daybreak until noon! They craved the historical accounts, laws, and covenant that had set them apart as God's Holy nation from the very beginning.

Well, I have made good use of the tissue box sitting nearby. I pray God will give me the supernatural ability to relay this in a way that grips us as deeply as it should. Our American culture may struggle to grasp a war-torn country such as this. And while this is not a perfect representation, I want to take you on a short journey with me in an attempt to comprehend what is happening.

Imagine our American soil has been attacked and taken over by another nation. The White House has been overthrown, and a new regime has set up its reign inside our nation's capital. What if our national anthem was forbidden and replaced with one we could not even understand? Our American culture would all be replaced by the culture and customs of our occupier. We would no longer be able to do what we wanted, eat what we wanted, or worship God like we wanted. Imagine years passing without being able to say the Pledge of Allegiance or see the red, white, and blue flying on flag poles. We would be a laughingstock amongst the nations and at the mercy of the new government.

Now skipping the make-believe details, let's say seventy years later, we have regained power over the nation. Really imagine this…the hour has come. Every man, woman, and child has found a television screen to crowd around. Every channel is broadcasting this one monumental moment. Walking out onto the White House balcony is the new president of the United States of America. He approaches the podium, an extreme hush falls over 3,794,083 square miles of American soil. "The Star-Spangled Banner" rings out in the background, played by a lone soldier on a trumpet. Many of the young people are hearing our national anthem for the very first time. To the right, the American flag slowly ascends up the silver flagpole. The wind catches it at the top and sends it billowing open; the stars and stripes vibrantly displayed for all to see. Veterans everywhere salute the flag for their country and for those who have died defending it. The older generations begin placing their right hand over their heart. Small children look up to the faces of their parents, teary-eyed, singing the national anthem. All of the people weep as one man.

THAT, dear one, is a tiny example of what is happening in Nehemiah chapter 8.

To the Israelites, the book of the Law was filled with long lost words of a once cherished foundation. What was scarcely a memory was now being proclaimed out loud as they recommitted their hearts to the One True God. What their ancestors refused to hear and obey, ultimately causing their destruction

> They did not simply resurrect stones for stones sake! They were resurrecting their devotion to God. Amen!

and exile, was now being read out loud to an eager, weeping, humbled nation. They did not simply resurrect stones for stones sake! They were resurrecting their devotion to God. Amen!

Take a moment to sit with those things in mind before you read Chapter 8:7–18.

7 The Levites-Jeshua, Bani, Sherebiah, Jamin, Akkub, Shabbethai, Hodiah, Maaseiah, Kelita, Azariah, Jozabad, Hanan and Pelaiah-instructed the people in the Law while the people were standing there. 8 They read from the Book of the Law of God, making it clear[1] and giving the meaning so that the people understood what was being read. 9 Then Nehemiah the governor, Ezra the priest and teacher of the Law, and the Levites who were instructing the people said to them all, "This day is holy to the Lord your God. Do not mourn or weep." For all the people had been weeping as they listened to the words of the Law. 10 Nehemiah said, "Go and enjoy choice food and sweet drinks, and send some to those who have nothing prepared. This day is holy to our Lord. Do not grieve, for the joy of the Lord is your strength." 11 The Levites calmed all the people, saying, "Be still, for this is a holy day. Do not grieve." 12 Then all the people went away to eat and drink, to send portions of food and to celebrate with great joy, because they now understood the words that had been made known to them. 13 On the second day of the month, the heads of all the families, along with the priests and the Levites, gathered around Ezra the teacher to give attention to the words of the Law. 14 They found written in the Law, which the Lord had commanded through Moses, that the Israelites were to live in temporary shelters during the festival of the seventh month 15 and that they should proclaim this word and spread it throughout their towns and in Jerusalem: "Go out into the hill country and bring back branches from olive and wild olive trees, and from myrtles, palms and shade trees, to make temporary shelters"-as it is written.[2] 16 So the people went out and brought back branches and built themselves temporary shelters on their own roofs, in their courtyards, in the courts of the house of God and in the square by the Water Gate and the one by the Gate of Ephraim. 17 The whole company that had returned from exile built temporary shelters and lived in them. From the days of Joshua son of Nun until that day, the Israelites had not celebrated it like this. And their joy was very great. 18 Day after day, from the first day to the last, Ezra read from the Book of the Law of God. They celebrated the festival for seven days, and on the eighth day, in accordance with the regulation, there was an assembly.

Key Points

- The priests instructed and taught the people from scripture, making it clear and giving it meaning so the people could understand.
- Nehemiah calls for the mourning period to end and to now rejoice.
- He establishes the day as a sacred one to celebrate together.
- They celebrate the fact that the hidden words of the law had now been made known to them.
- The people begin to follow the instructions given in the law.
- Day after day Ezra read out loud from the book of the law of God.
- And the people listened and celebrated for seven straight days.

Their hunger to reestablish God as supreme over their lives revolved around the devouring of His word. They stood listening for hours each day. NO OTHER book ever penned could ever command such an audience with as much power!

NO OTHER book ever penned could ever command such an audience with as much power!

"For the word of God is alive and active. Sharper than any double-edged sword, it penetrates even to dividing soul and spirit, joint and marrow; it judges thoughts and attitudes of the heart" (Hebrews 4:12).

"All scripture is God breathed and is useful for teaching, rebuking, correcting, and training in righteousness, so that the servant of God may be thoroughly equipped for every good work" (2 Timothy 3:16–17).

Praise the Lord! The Scriptures we hold in our hands today are "alive and active," fully relevant to us in our time here on earth. May we have the same awe and longing to hear it spoken over our own lives.

We have read through this biblical account from rubble to fortified fortress. What was nearly desolate is now inhabited. Hearts of disobedience were exchanged for hearts of repentance. We have seen God bring beauty from ashes. Let us go into our personal rebuilding time full of the same hope.

Personal Rebuilding

What about your walls? In what ways, no matter how small, do you see progress in your rebuilding?

_____

_____

_____

_____

We may not be able to stand on our kitchen tables and read the entire Bible to our families in one sitting, but how can you commit to making God's word relevant in your home?

_____

_____

_____

What particular scripture do you need to have READ OVER you and your home? Jot it down below and make a point to share it out loud with a family member.

_____

_____

_____

There is no denying that this is heavy material, and you have done a lot of hard work. So guess what? Now it is time to celebrate! Nehemiah called for a time of mourning to cease so they could refresh themselves and enjoy fellowship. So will you!

It is your turn to take a break from the hard stuff to enjoy the beautiful pieces. You need to make a plan to celebrate! Be creative and make it specifically meaningful to you. Go out for coffee with a friend. Bless yourself with a nap if you need to refuel. Go for a long walk with just you and the Lord. Whatever it may be that would most bless you, commit to taking time away from the heaviness of rebuilding and celebrate your progress.

Write your plan below so that you make yourself do it.

_____

_____

_____

_____

_____

Let God sing over you with His love and His ability to rebuild in your life.

 "Love Is Rebuilding Us" by Jason Gray

Confession and Renewal

Nehemiah and the people are about to review the details of their family tree and history as God's people. Not all of it will be good, but it will be for good reason. Before we think this portion of scripture does not directly apply to us, let us keep in mind the Israelites are not the only ones who have some shady areas tucked in their family ancestry.

To attest to this truth, I will share an interesting story I uncovered regarding my own ancestors. It is quite intriguing.

One day, I came across a certain black-and-white photograph that hung on my grandmother's wall. The photo contained an old woman surrounded by her five grown children. I asked my grandma about it and was surprised to learn that she only knew the children's names. There was no one left alive who could tell us the mother's name.

The old woman's face stayed in my mind even weeks later. It bothered me that over the years, she had simply been forgotten, hanging there behind the glass—nameless. Feeling a personal sense of loss over this fact, I began a determined hunt for answers online. I combed through pages and pages of immigration records. I learned that her husband, Stanislaw, had come to America in 1903 to pave the way for her and their children.

Searching for this woman was a needle in a haystack search for sure, but one that seemed possible due to the fact my grandmother knew the names of all five children. And guess what? I found them! All five names and accurate ages were scribbled by hand onto the official Immigration Registry.

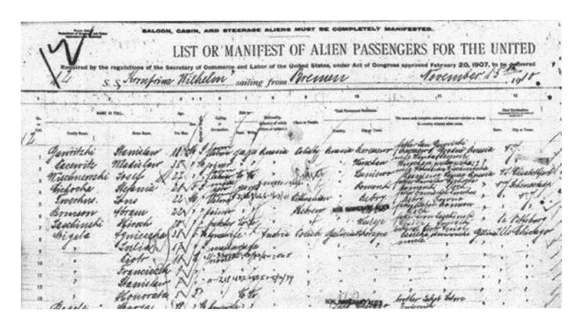

I was absolutely THRILLED! Written directly above the names of each child was the long-lost name of my great-great-great-grandmother…Agneszeika! More than likely, her name would have been shortened to Agnes once she arrived here in the states. I was unbelievably excited to share this information with my grandma and all my aunts and uncles whom I was keeping apprised of my search findings.

There was just one small problem. Agneszeika arrived to the United States in 1910 to be reunited with her husband who had been gone for seven years. Upon her arrival, the ages of the children with her were seventeen, eleven, nine, seven, and three years old. I am sure it won't take you long to do the math! It's possible she was pregnant with their fourth child when he left, but she also had a three-year-old! I was stunned! So while I had intended to save this woman from the fate of remaining nameless, I had, in fact, stumbled upon details she may have preferred remained buried. With no further avenue to investigate the new timeline discrepancy, all I could do was relay the facts as they were to the rest of my family.

Now I will never know the full story behind the possible family scandal that I unearthed. Maybe there is a perfectly good explanation, but one thing is certain. We all have family trees littered with the good and bad of those who have gone before us. It was no different for the people of God.

Take your time with this next section of scripture. This is a valuable overview of the entire Old Testament up to this point in history. The overseers of the rebuilding project are detailing out the good and bad of the history between themselves and their God, in particular, the ways their ancestors had failed to obey God. Read Chapter 9:1–38.

Ezra's Confession of Israel's Sins

9 1 On the twenty-fourth day of the same month, the Israelites gathered together, fasting and wearing sackcloth and putting dust on their heads. **2** Those of Israelite descent had separated themselves from all foreigners. They stood in their places and confessed their sins and the sins of their ancestors. **3** They stood where they were and read from the Book of the Law of the Lord their God for a quarter of the day, and spent another quarter in confession and in worshiping the Lord their God. **4** Standing on the stairs of the Levites were Jeshua, Bani, Kadmiel, Shebaniah, Bunni, Sherebiah, Bani and Kenani. They cried out with loud voices to the Lord their God. **5** And the Levites-Jeshua, Kadmiel, Bani, Hashabneiah, Sherebiah, Hodiah, Shebaniah and Pethahiah-said: "Stand up and praise the Lord your God, who is from everlasting to everlasting.[1]" "Blessed be your glorious name, and may it be exalted above all blessing and praise. **6** You alone are the Lord. You made the heavens, even the highest heavens, and all their starry host, the earth and all that is on it, the seas and all that is in them. You give life to everything, and the multitudes of heaven worship you. **7** "You are the LordGod, who chose Abram and brought him out of Ur of the Chaldeans and named him Abraham. **8** You found his heart faithful to you, and you made a covenant with him to give to his descendants the land of the Canaanites, Hittites, Amorites, Perizzites, Jebusites and Girgashites. You have kept your promise because you are righteous. **9** "You saw the suffering of our ancestors in Egypt; you heard their cry at the Red Sea.[2] **10** You sent signs and wonders against Pharaoh, against all his officials and all the people of his land, for you knew how arrogantly the Egyptians treated them. You made a name for yourself, which remains to this day. **11** You divided the sea before them, so that they passed through it on dry ground, but you hurled their pursuers into the depths, like a stone into mighty waters. **12** By day you led them with a pillar of cloud, and by night with a pillar of fire to give them light on the way they were to take. **13** "You came down on Mount Sinai; you spoke to them from heaven. You gave them regulations and laws that are just and right, and decrees and commands that are good. **14** You made known to them your holy Sabbath and gave them commands, decrees and laws through your servant Moses. **15** In their hunger you gave them bread from heaven and in their thirst you brought them water from the rock; you told them to go in and take possession of the land you had sworn with uplifted hand to give them. **16** "But they, our ancestors, became arrogant and stiff-necked, and they did not obey your commands. **17** They refused to listen and failed to remember the miracles you performed among them. They became stiff-necked and in their rebellion appointed a leader in order to return to their slavery. But you are a forgiving God, gracious and compassionate, slow to anger and abounding in love. Therefore you did not desert them, **18** even when they cast for themselves an image of a calf and said, 'This is your god, who brought you up out of Egypt,' or when they committed awful blasphemies. **19** "Because of your great compassion you did not abandon them in the wilderness. By day the pillar of cloud did not fail to guide them on their path, nor the pillar of fire by night to shine on the way they were to take. **20** You gave your good Spirit to instruct them. You did not withhold your manna from their mouths, and you gave them water for their thirst. **21** For forty years you sustained them in the wilderness; they lacked nothing, their clothes did not wear out nor did their feet become swollen. **22** "You gave them kingdoms and nations, allotting to them even the remotest frontiers. They took over the country of Sihon[3] king of Heshbon and the country of Og king of Bashan. **23** You made their children as numerous as the stars in the sky, and you brought them into the land that you told their parents to enter and possess. **24** Their children went in and took possession of the land. You subdued before them the

Canaanites, who lived in the land; you gave the Canaanites into their hands, along with their kings and the peoples of the land, to deal with them as they pleased. **25** They captured fortified cities and fertile land; they took possession of houses filled with all kinds of good things, wells already dug, vineyards, olive groves and fruit trees in abundance. They ate to the full and were well-nourished; they reveled in your great goodness. **26** "But they were disobedient and rebelled against you; they turned their backs on your law. They killed your prophets, who had warned them in order to turn them back to you; they committed awful blasphemies. **27** So you delivered them into the hands of their enemies, who oppressed them. But when they were oppressed they cried out to you. From heaven you heard them, and in your great compassion you gave them deliverers, who rescued them from the hand of their enemies. **28** "But as soon as they were at rest, they again did what was evil in your sight. Then you abandoned them to the hand of their enemies so that they ruled over them. And when they cried out to you again, you heard from heaven, and in your compassion you delivered them time after time. **29** "You warned them in order to turn them back to your law, but they became arrogant and disobeyed your commands. They sinned against your ordinances, of which you said, 'The person who obeys them will live by them.' Stubbornly they turned their backs on you, became stiff-necked and refused to listen. **30** For many years you were patient with them. By your Spirit you warned them through your prophets. Yet they paid no attention, so you gave them into the hands of the neighboring peoples. **31** But in your great mercy you did not put an end to them or abandon them, for you are a gracious and merciful God. **32** "Now therefore, our God, the great God, mighty and awesome, who keeps his covenant of love, do not let all this hardship seem trifling in your eyes-the hardship that has come on us, on our kings and leaders, on our priests and prophets, on our ancestors and all your people, from the days of the kings of Assyria until today. **33** In all that has happened to us, you have remained righteous; you have acted faithfully, while we acted wickedly. **34** Our kings, our leaders, our priests and our ancestors did not follow your law; they did not pay attention to your commands or the statutes you warned them to keep. **35** Even while they were in their kingdom, enjoying your great goodness to them in the spacious and fertile land you gave them, they did not serve you or turn from their evil ways. **36** "But see, we are slaves today, slaves in the land you gave our ancestors so they could eat its fruit and the other good things it produces. **37** Because of our sins, its abundant harvest goes to the kings you have placed over us. They rule over our bodies and our cattle as they please. We are in great distress.

The People Covenant to Keep the Law

38 "In view of all this, we are making a binding agreement, putting it in writing, and our leaders, our Levites and our priests are affixing their seals to it."

Key Points

- Part of mourning was a time of deep and full confession on behalf of their people.
- Then they spent time REVIEWING THEIR HISTORY WITH GOD. The cycle of disobedience and rebellion to God's correction and mercy.
- He ends the chapter by writing up a binding agreement and the leaders all signed it.

Take a moment to look back over chapter 9:16–31 when he is reviewing their rebellious history with God. Write down words used to describe the actions of the Israelites versus the actions of God. I will even get you started with one listed in each.

ISRAELITES' ACTIONS	GOD'S ACTIONS
STIFF-NECKED	GRACIOUS

Amazing, isn't it? His love and graciousness remain even when His children turn from Him time and time again. It reminds me of another verse found in the New Testament that has a similar truth.

"If we are faithless, he will remain faithful, for he cannot disown himself" (2 Timothy 2:13).

A couple more things I want to point out in this large portion of verses. Jot down the key elements missing.

Verse 17—They refused to _____ and failed to _____ .

In their rebellion, they appointed a leader in order to return to their _____ .

Verse 26—They turned their backs to _____ .

Verse 28—But as soon as they were at _____ they again did evil in your sight.

When you read those few verses, did you grasp an incredible reality?
THIS IS THE WHOLE REASON THEY WERE IN RUINS IN THE FIRST PLACE!
Hear this, loved one, **FORGETTING** God leads to **COMPLACENCY,** which then leads to **SIN. SIN** requires godly **DISCIPLINE!**
The sole aim of godly **DISCIPLINE** is to bring you to **REPENTANCE** so that you can experience **RESTORATION!**
It seems so obvious to us, doesn't it? We may even be tempted to think the Israelites are a foolish people who really needed to get their act together. In reality, the people of our day, you and me, are really no different. In our blessings, we can ease into comfortable and predictable lives. We then depend upon Him less and less until we operate fairly self-sufficiently. We then begin to bend rules and blur lines because we forget the

seriousness of the Lord's commands. If we continue in our sin, God will lovingly but firmly bring discipline to draw us back to Himself.

"Because the LORD disciplines those he loves" (Proverbs 3:12).

Dear one, know that if you have experienced or are currently experiencing this kind of discipline, it is LOVE that drives your Heavenly Father. He longs to draw you into safe places. He does not want you to be lulled to sleep by complacency.

Personal Rebuilding

Look back at page 67. Fill in the blanks below with the BOLD truth of chapter 9.

_____ God leads to _____ , which then leads to _____ . _____ requires _____ ! The sole aim of Godly _____ is to bring you to _____ so that you can experience _____ .

Does this cycle strike you as painfully obvious, but still you find yourself falling into similar patterns? Do not be overwhelmed with shame, loved one, for this is the plight of all humanity. We are sinful at our very core, which means we will continually fight the desires of our flesh. We will mess up from time to time. That is the whole reason Jesus Christ came to live a perfect life and die in our place. He knows we are helpless to save ourselves, both in Nehemiah's time and now in our time. So what can we do? Continue to seek Him. And when we fail, accept His undeserved mercy as He picks us up and sends us out again.

In the text we read in Nehemiah, did you notice the importance of beginning with confession and ending with a binding agreement? They were so desperate to not slip into old patterns of dismissing God that they wanted to mark it as a new day.

The next page provided is for you to write your own binding agreement. Write down a summary of your rebuilding journey so far. Look back over previous personal rebuilding sessions to remind yourself of where you started, what you have learned, and where you see God leading. Please view this step as a powerful covenantal turning point between you and the Lord. When you finish writing it, <u>wait</u> <u>to</u> <u>sign</u> <u>it</u> <u>until</u> <u>instructed</u> <u>to</u> <u>do</u> <u>so</u> <u>in</u> <u>the</u> <u>last</u> <u>chapter.</u>

Spend time hearing God sing over you with this powerful song.

 "God's Not Done with You" by Tauren Wells

Heavenly Father,

_____
_____
_____
_____
_____
_____
_____
_____
_____
_____
_____
_____
_____
_____
_____
_____
_____
_____
_____
_____
_____
_____
_____
_____
_____
_____
_____

God, I lay all this at your feet and before your throne. Would you empower me to walk it by your Holy Spirit? It is my desire to honor these words and walk in your grace and mercy as I am being made new day by day.

Date _____ Signature _____

LESSON 8

Dedication of the Wall

You made it! You have trudged through heavy material to make your way to the FINAL chapters of Nehemiah. I am genuinely thankful for your perseverance! Now please bear with me as we read through the last three chapters as larger chunks of reading. Then we will wrap it all up with the highlights of Nehemiah.

Please read all of Chapter 10.

10 1 Those who sealed it were: Nehemiah the governor, the son of Hakaliah. Zedekiah, **2** Seraiah, Azariah, Jeremiah, **3** Pashhur, Amariah, Malkijah, **4** Hattush, Shebaniah, Malluk, **5** Harim, Meremoth, Obadiah, **6** Daniel, Ginnethon, Baruch, **7** Meshullam, Abijah, Mijamin, **8** Maaziah, Bilgai and Shemaiah. These were the priests. **9** The Levites: Jeshua son of Azaniah, Binnui of the sons of Henadad, Kadmiel, **10** and their associates: Shebaniah, Hodiah, Kelita, Pelaiah, Hanan, **11** Mika, Rehob, Hashabiah, **12** Zakkur, Sherebiah, Shebaniah, **13** Hodiah, Bani and Beninu. **14** The leaders of the people: Parosh, Pahath-Moab, Elam, Zattu, Bani, **15** Bunni, Azgad, Bebai, **16** Adonijah, Bigvai, Adin, **17** Ater, Hezekiah, Azzur, **18** Hodiah, Hashum, Bezai, **19** Hariph, Anathoth, Nebai, **20** Magpiash, Meshullam, Hezir, **21** Meshezabel, Zadok, Jaddua, **22** Pelatiah, Hanan, Anaiah, **23** Hoshea, Hananiah, Hasshub, **24** Hallohesh, Pilha, Shobek, **25** Rehum, Hashabnah, Maaseiah, **26** Ahiah, Hanan, Anan, **27** Malluk, Harim and Baanah. **28** "The rest of the people-priests, Levites, gatekeepers, musicians, temple servants and all who separated themselves from the neighboring peoples for the sake of the Law of God, together with their wives and all their sons and daughters who are able to understand—**29** all these now join their fellow Israelites the nobles, and bind themselves with a curse and an oath to follow the Law of God given through Moses the servant of God and to obey carefully all the commands, regulations and decrees of the Lord our Lord. **30** "We promise not to give our daughters in marriage to the peoples around us or take their daughters for our sons. **31** "When the neighboring peoples bring merchandise or grain to sell on the Sabbath, we will not buy from them on the Sabbath or on any holy day. Every seventh year we will forgo working the land and will cancel all debts. **32** "We assume the responsibility for carrying out the commands to give a third of a shekel[1] each year for the service of the house of our God: **33** for the bread set out on the table; for the regular grain offerings and burnt offerings; for the offerings on the Sabbaths, at the New Moon feasts and at the appointed festivals; for the holy offerings; for sin offerings [2] to make atonement for Israel; and for all the duties of the house of our God. **34** "We-the priests, the Levites and the people-have cast lots to determine when each of our families is to bring to the house of our God at set times each year a contribution of wood to burn on the altar of the Lord our God, as it is written in the Law. **35** "We also assume responsibility for bringing to the house of the Lord each year the firstfruits of our crops and of every fruit tree. **36** "As it is also written in the Law, we will bring the firstborn of our sons and of our cattle, of our herds and of our flocks to the house of our God, to the priests ministering there. **37** "Moreover, we will bring to the storerooms of the house of our God, to the priests, the first of our ground meal, of our grain offerings, of the fruit of all our trees and of our new wine and olive oil. And we will bring a tithe of our crops to the Levites, for it is the Levites who collect the tithes in all the towns where we work. **38** A priest descended from Aaron is to accompany the Levites when they receive the tithes, and the Levites are to bring a tenth of the tithes up to the house of our God, to the storerooms of the treasury. **39** The people of Israel, including the Levites, are to bring their contributions of grain, new wine and olive oil to the storerooms, where the articles for the sanctuary and for the ministering priests, the gatekeepers and the musicians are also kept. "We will not neglect the house of our God."

Key Points

- Nehemiah lists those present at the sealing of the document they had all signed.
- He recommits them all to the commands, regulations, and decrees that were given to God's people from the beginning.

Please read all of chapter 11.

The Residents of Jerusalem

11 1 Now the leaders of the people settled in Jerusalem. The rest of the people cast lots to bring one out of every ten of them to live in Jerusalem, the holy city, while the remaining nine were to stay in their own towns. **2** The people commended all who volunteered to live in Jerusalem. **3** These are the provincial leaders who settled in Jerusalem (now some Israelites, priests, Levites, temple servants and descendants of Solomon's servants lived in the towns of Judah, each on their own property in the various towns, **4** while other people from both Judah and Benjamin lived in Jerusalem): From the descendants of Judah: Athaiah son of Uzziah, the son of Zechariah, the son of Amariah, the son of Shephatiah, the son of Mahalalel, a descendant of Perez; **5** and Maaseiah son of Baruch, the son of Kol-Hozeh, the son of Hazaiah, the son of Adaiah, the son of Joiarib, the son of Zechariah, a descendant of Shelah. **6** The descendants of Perez who lived in Jerusalem totaled 468 men of standing. **7** From the descendants of Benjamin: Sallu son of Meshullam, the son of Joed, the son of Pedaiah, the son of Kolaiah, the son of Maaseiah, the son of Ithiel, the son of Jeshaiah, **8** and his followers, Gabbai and Sallai-928 men. **9** Joel son of Zikri was their chief officer, and Judah son of Hassenuah was over the New Quarter of the city. **10** From the priests: Jedaiah; the son of Joiarib; Jakin; **11** Seraiah son of Hilkiah, the son of Meshullam, the son of Zadok, the son of Meraioth, the son of Ahitub, the official in charge of the house of God, **12** and their associates, who carried on work for the temple-822 men; Adaiah son of Jeroham, the son of Pelaliah, the son of Amzi, the son of Zechariah, the son of Pashhur, the son of Malkijah, **13** and his associates, who were heads of families-242 men; Amashsai son of Azarel, the son of Ahzai, the son of Meshillemoth, the son of Immer, **14** and his[1]associates, who were men of standing-128. Their chief officer was Zabdiel son of Haggedolim. **15** From the Levites: Shemaiah son of Hasshub, the son of Azrikam, the son of Hashabiah, the son of Bunni; **16** Shabbethai and Jozabad, two of the heads of the Levites, who had charge of the outside work of the house of God; **17** Mattaniah son of Mika, the son of Zabdi, the son of Asaph, the director who led in thanksgiving and prayer; Bakbukiah, second among his associates; and Abda son of Shammua, the son of Galal, the son of Jeduthun. **18** The Levites in the holy city totaled 284. **19** The gatekeepers: Akkub, Talmon and their associates, who kept watch at the gates-172 men. **20** The rest of the Israelites, with the priests and Levites, were in all the towns of Judah, each on their ancestral property. **21** The temple servants lived on the hill of Ophel, and Ziha and Gishpa were in charge of them. **22** The chief officer of the Levites in Jerusalem was Uzzi son of Bani, the son of Hashabiah, the son of Mattaniah, the son of Mika. Uzzi was one of Asaph's descendants, who were the musicians responsible for the service of the house of God. **23** The musicians were under the king's orders, which regulated their daily activity. **24** Pethahiah son of Meshezabel, one of the descendants of Zerah son of Judah, was the king's agent in all affairs relating to the people.

The Settlement outside of Jerusalem

25 As for the villages with their fields, some of the people of Judah lived in Kiriath Arba and its surrounding settlements, in Dibon and its settlements, in Jekabzeel and its villages, **26** in Jeshua, in Moladah, in Beth Pelet, **27** in Hazar Shual, in Beersheba and its settlements, **28** in Ziklag, in Mekonah and its settlements, **29** in En Rimmon, in Zorah, in Jarmuth, **30** Zanoah, Adullam and their villages, in Lachish and its fields, and in Azekah and its settlements. So they were living all the way from Beersheba to the Valley of Hinnom. **31** The descendants of the Benjamites from Geba lived in Mikmash, Aija, Bethel and its settlements, **32** in Anathoth, Nob and Ananiah, **33** in Hazor, Ramah and Gittaim, **34** in Hadid, Zeboim and Neballat, **35** in Lod and Ono, and in Ge Harashim. **36** Some of the divisions of the Levites of Judah settled in Benjamin.

Key Points

- The leaders who were assigned over Jerusalem settled inside the city.
- They established a lottery system for the remaining available occupancy.
- They record in detail what families of what tribes and how many settled within the city.
- The rest of the Israelites were given back their ancestral property outside the city in the surrounding towns.

Please read chapter 12:1–26.

The Priests and Levites

12 1 These were the priests and Levites who returned with Zerubbabel son of Shealtiel and with Joshua: Seraiah, Jeremiah, Ezra, **2** Amariah, Malluk, Hattush, **3** Shekaniah, Rehum, Meremoth, **4** Iddo, Ginnethon, [1] Abijah, **5** Mijamin, [2] Moadiah, Bilgah, **6** Shemaiah, Joiarib, Jedaiah, **7** Sallu, Amok, Hilkiah and Jedaiah. These were the leaders of the priests and their associates in the days of Joshua. **8** The Levites were Jeshua, Binnui, Kadmiel, Sherebiah, Judah, and also Mattaniah, who, together with his associates, was in charge of the songs of thanksgiving. **9** Bakbukiah and Unni, their associates, stood opposite them in the services. **10** Joshua was the father of Joiakim, Joiakim the father of Eliashib, Eliashib the father of Joiada, **11** Joiada the father of Jonathan, and Jonathan the father of Jaddua. **12** In the days of Joiakim, these were the heads of the priestly families: of Seraiah's family, Meraiah; of Jeremiah's, Hananiah; **13** of Ezra's, Meshullam; of Amariah's, Jehohanan; **14** of Malluk's, Jonathan; of Shekaniah's, [3]Joseph; **15** of Harim's, Adna; of Meremoth's, [4] Haikai; **16** of Iddo's, Zechariah; of Ignition's, Meshullam; **17** of Abijah's, Zikri; of Miniamin's and of Moadiah's, Piltai; **18** of Bilgah's, Shammua; of Shemaiah's, Jehonathan; **19** of Joiarib's, Mattenai; of Jedaiah's, Uzzi; **20** of Sallu's, Kallai; of Amok's, Eber; **21** of Hilkiah's, Hashabiah; of Jedaiah's, Nethanel. **22** The family heads of the Levites in the days of Eliashib, Joiada, Johanan and Jaddua, as well as those of the priests, were recorded in the reign of Darius the Persian. **23** The family heads among the descendants of Levi up to the time of Johanan son of Eliashib were recorded in the book of the annals. **24** And the leaders of the Levites were Hashabiah, Sherebiah, Jeshua son of Kadmiel, and their associates, who stood opposite them to give praise and thanksgiving, one section responding to the other, as prescribed by David the man of God. **25** Mattaniah, Bakbukiah, Obadiah, Meshullam, Talmon and Akkub were gatekeepers who guarded the storerooms at the gates. **26** They served in the days of Joiakim son of Joshua, the son of Jozadak, and in the days of Nehemiah the governor and of Ezra the priest, the teacher of the Law.

Key Points

- The Levites were the chosen line out of the twelve tribes of Israel to be set apart as priests.
- Nehemiah records the priests and Levites who returned to the land.

Please read chapter 12:27–47.

The Dedication of the Wall

27 At the dedication of the wall of Jerusalem, the Levites were sought out from where they lived and were brought to Jerusalem to celebrate joyfully the dedication with songs of thanksgiving and with the music of cymbals, harps and lyres. **28** The musicians also were brought together from the region around Jerusalem-from the villages of the Netophathites, **29** from Beth Gilgal, and from the area of Geba and Azmaveth, for the musicians had built villages for themselves around Jerusalem. **30** When the priests and Levites had purified themselves ceremonially, they purified the people, the gates and the wall. **31** I had the leaders of Judah go up on top of[5] the wall. I also assigned two large choirs to give thanks. One was to proceed on top of[6] the wall to the right, toward the Dung Gate. **32** Hoshaiah and half the leaders of Judah followed them, **33** along with Azariah, Ezra, Meshullam, **34** Judah, Benjamin, Shemaiah, Jeremiah, **35** as well as some priests with trumpets, and also Zechariah son of Jonathan, the son of Shemaiah, the son of Mattaniah, the son of Micaiah, the son of Zakkur, the son of Asaph, **36** and his associates-Shemaiah, Azarel, Milalai, Gilalai, Maai, Nethanel, Judah and Hanani-with musical instruments prescribed by David the man of God. Ezra the teacher of the Law led the procession. **37** At the Fountain Gate they continued directly up the steps of the City of David on the ascent to the wall and passed above the site of David's palace to the Water Gate on the east. **38** The second choir proceeded in the opposite direction. I followed them on top of[7] the wall, together with half the people-past the Tower of the Ovens to the Broad Wall, **39** over the Gate of Ephraim, the Jeshanah[8] Gate, the Fish Gate, the Tower of Hananel and the Tower of the Hundred, as far as the Sheep Gate. At the Gate of the Guard they stopped. **40** The two choirs that gave thanks then took their places in the house of God; so did I, together with half the officials, **41** as well as the priests-Eliakim, Maaseiah, Miniamin, Micaiah, Elioenai, Zechariah and Hananiah with their trumpets-**42** and also Maaseiah, Shemaiah, Eleazar, Uzzi, Jehohanan, Malkijah, Elam and Ezer. The choirs sang under the direction of Jezrahiah. **43** And on that day they offered great sacrifices, rejoicing because God had given them great joy. The women and children also rejoiced. The sound of rejoicing in Jerusalem could be heard far away.

The Provision for the Priests and Levites

44 At that time men were appointed to be in charge of the storerooms for the contributions, firstfruits and tithes. From the fields around the towns they were to bring into the storerooms the portions required by the Law for the priests and the Levites, for Judah was pleased with the ministering priests and Levites. **45** They performed the service of their God and the service of purification, as did also the musicians and gatekeepers, according to the commands of David and his son Solomon. **46** For long ago, in the days of David and Asaph, there had been directors for the musicians and for the songs of praise and thanksgiving to God. **47** So in the days of Zerubbabel and of Nehemiah, all Israel contributed the daily portions for the musicians and the gatekeepers. They also set aside the portion for the other Levites, and the Levites set aside the portion for the descendants of Aaron

Key Points

- The wall has been dedicated.
- The priest ceremonially purified themselves, all the people, the gates, and the walls.
- There was a joyous celebration, filled with musical processions around the entire wall. They ended at the house of God where they offered great sacrifices to Him.
- Men were appointed to oversee the storehouses and tithes, governing them as in the days of King David.

The end of verse 43 is my favorite! Look at it again and fill it in on the next page.
The sound of rejoicing in Jerusalem could be _____ .
What a testimony to those far away that the rejoicing of God's people carried over the miles to reach their ears.

Please read the final chapter of Nehemiah, chapter 13.

Nehemiah's Reforms

13 1 On that day the Book of Moses was read aloud in the hearing of the people and there it was found written that no Ammonite or Moabite should ever be admitted into the assembly of God, **2** because they had not met the Israelites with food and water but had hired Balaam to call a curse down on them. (Our God, however, turned the curse into a blessing.) **3** When the people heard this law, they excluded from Israel all who were of foreign descent. **4** Before this, Eliashib the priest had been put in charge of the storerooms of the house of our God. He was closely associated with Tobiah, **5** and he had provided him with a large room formerly used to store the grain offerings and incense and temple articles, and also the tithes of grain, new wine and olive oil prescribed for the Levites, musicians and gatekeepers, as well as the contributions for the priests. **6** But while all this was going on, I was not in Jerusalem, for in the thirty-second year of Artaxerxes king of Babylon I had returned to the king. Some time later I asked his permission **7** and came back to Jerusalem. Here I learned about the evil thing Eliashib had done in providing Tobiah a room in the courts of the house of God. **8** I was greatly displeased and threw all Tobiah's household goods out of the room. **9** I gave orders to purify the rooms, and then I put back into them the equipment of the house of God, with the grain offerings and the incense. **10** I also learned that the portions assigned to the Levites had not been given to them, and that all the Levites and musicians responsible for the service had gone back to their own fields. **11** So I rebuked the officials and asked them, "Why is the house of God neglected?" Then I called them together and stationed them at their posts. **12** All Judah brought the tithes of grain, new wine and olive oil into the storerooms. **13** I put Shelemiah the priest, Zadok the scribe, and a Levite named Pedaiah in charge of the storerooms and made Hanan son of Zakkur, the son of Mattaniah, their assistant, because they were considered trustworthy. They were made responsible for distributing the supplies to their fellow Levites. **14** Remember me for this, my God, and do not blot out what I have so faithfully done for the house of my God and its services. **15** In those days I saw people in Judah treading winepresses on the Sabbath and bringing in grain and loading it on donkeys, together with wine, grapes, figs and all other kinds of loads. And they were bringing all this into Jerusalem on the Sabbath. Therefore I warned them against selling food on that day. **16** People from Tyre who lived in Jerusalem were bringing in fish and all kinds of merchandise and selling them in Jerusalem on the Sabbath to the people of Judah. **17** I rebuked the nobles of Judah and said to them, "What is this wicked thing you are doing-desecrating the Sabbath day? **18** Didn't your ancestors do the same things, so that our God brought all this calamity on us and on this city? Now you are stirring up more wrath against Israel by desecrating the Sabbath." **19** When evening shadows fell on the gates of Jerusalem before the Sabbath, I ordered the doors to be shut and not opened until the Sabbath was over. I stationed some of my own men at the gates so that no load could be brought in on the Sabbath day. **20** Once or twice the merchants and sellers of all kinds of goods spent the night outside Jerusalem. **21** But I warned them and said, "Why do you spend the night by the wall? If you do this again, I will arrest you." From that time on they no longer came on the Sabbath. **22** Then I commanded the Levites to purify themselves and go and guard the gates in order to keep the Sabbath day holy. Remember me for this also, my God, and show mercy to me according to your great love. **23** Moreover, in those days I saw men of Judah who had married women from Ashdod, Ammon and Moab. **24** Half of their children spoke the language of Ashdod or the language of one of the other peoples, and did not know how to speak the language of Judah.

25 I rebuked them and called curses down on them. I beat some of the men and pulled out their hair. I made them take an oath in God's name and said: "You are not to give your daughters in marriage to their sons, nor are you to take their daughters in marriage for your sons or for your-selves. **26** Was it not because of marriages like these that Solomon king of Israel sinned? Among the many nations there was no king like him. He was loved by his God, and God made him king over all Israel, but even he was led into sin by foreign women. **27** Must we hear now that you too are doing all this terrible wickedness and are being unfaithful to our God by marrying foreign women?" **28** One of the sons of Joiada son of Eliashib the high priest was son-in-law to Sanballat the Horonite. And I drove him away from me. **29** Remember them, my God, because they defiled the priestly office and the covenant of the priesthood and of the Levites. **30** So I purified the priests and the Levites of everything foreign, and assigned them duties, each to his own task. **31** I also made provision for contributions of wood at designated times, and for the firstfruits. Remember me with favor, my God.

Key Points

- Twelve years have passed.
- Nehemiah left Jerusalem to return to the service of the king as he promised.
- Nehemiah goes to visit Jerusalem to find a few things are already amiss.
- Tobiah is using a large room in God's storehouse. Nehemiah kicks him out!
- The priests are not being provided for from the house of God as directed, so they needed to return to work their fields. Nehemiah fixes this and sets someone trustworthy to oversee the provisions from here on out.
- People were already disregarding the Sabbath as holy by working and bringing loads into the city on that day.
- Nehemiah shut the doors! He makes an amusing threat: "I will lay hands on you!"
- The people are marrying foreign women again. He rebukes them plainly and calls down curses on them. He even beat some of the men. He reminds them this is where the Israelites fell away from the Lord in the first place.

I know what you may be thinking, but before you chuck your Bible across the room in frustration with the Israelites, let's address some things.

First of all, we are ALL sinners, incapable of walking the straight and narrow very long before face-plant-ing. That is the curse of sin and why we need Jesus's death on the cross.

Secondly, a lot of time has passed. There has been a little over a decade between chapter 12 and chapter 13. While that does not give them an excuse for their actions, it does give us another glimpse into the sinful character of man. We are by nature forgetful of God, which is why He calls us to REMEMBER over and over again in scripture.

Lastly, once sin was identified, Nehemiah was clear and forceful to have it removed! There should be no mistake that he took serious action to eradicate the dangers of compromise leading the people into sin. We need to maintain the same level of vigilance over our own lives as we move into the years ahead God has for us.

Let's look at one final piece of this chapter before we move on.

Look at 13:14, the end of 13:22, 13:29, and the end of 13:31. What is repeated?

_____

He wants to be remembered with favor by God for all he has done. He has poured out his life and heart onto God's work, and he wants it to matter. I can relate to that! This life is HARD! Are you raising kids? HARD! Are you standing up for the weak? HARD! Are you struggling financially? HARD! Walking this life with the integrity of our faith is HARD loved one. We all want to know that what we do for His namesake matters!

It stirs in me this one question. When all is said and done and my life is over, what will my legacy be? What will bring honor to God as having had eternal significance?

This is one of the reasons why I like to write things down. I am not the best at journaling on a regular basis, but there have been times I have felt God prompt me to write out all of the details of a story to remember it and share it with my children. God directed me to this powerful verse in Psalms during one of those times. I was recording His sovereignty in the adoption of my son when this leapt off the pages of scripture…

"Let this be written for a future generation, that a people not yet created may praise the Lord," (Psalms 102:18).

A people not yet created? What a thrilling thought! The steps of obedient writing I do today could one day impact my children's children! I cannot even fathom it! But God can. And what each of us does today to rebuild walls, stand against opposition, and remember all God has done will spill over into generations to come! AMEN!

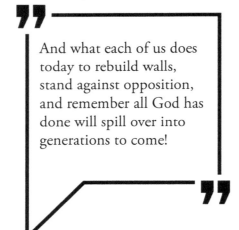

And what each of us does today to rebuild walls, stand against opposition, and remember all God has done will spill over into generations to come!

As we wrap up, permit me one last story I want to share with you about how personal your God can be.

Driving home one particular day, I was reeling with gloom and an inability to find joy in anything around me. Then I saw a sign for a flea market ahead and decided to stop in for a little "thrift shopping therapy." I wandered around the array of items, still feeling alone and unable to shake the pity party I had been throwing myself. I eventually came to stacks of old books to dig through. In truth, I am drawn to them not because I am an avid reader but because I like how they look and feel. I love the charm of them neatly arranged on a table or stacked on a windowsill.

I reached over to select one bright-red book in particular that caught my eye. The worn gold lettering on the front cover read "<u>Streams</u> <u>in</u> <u>the</u> <u>Desert</u>." Intrigued, I decided to actually open the book. I flipped through the pages and assessed that it was some sort of daily devotional. *Sure, but was it any good?* I thought sourly. I then did something I find quite embarrassing to admit, so try not to laugh. I proceeded to perform one of those small tests of God that no mature Christian should admit to. That's right, I flipped to that days reading, March11, as a test to see if it would grip me. God, in His mercy, did more than just indulge my juvenile test. Please read what I read that day…

March 11

Sorrow came to you yesterday, and emptied your home. Your first impulse now is to give up, and sit down in despair amid the wrecks of your hopes. But you dare not do it. You are in the line of battle, and the crisis is at hand. To falter a moment would be to imperil some holy interest. Other lives would be harmed by your pausing, holy interests would suffer, should your hands be folded. You must not linger even to indulge your grief.

I stood speechless.

I paid the man his quarter for the book and hurried to my van.

All was quiet, and I was alone.

I took a deep breath and reopened the book again to March 11. Conviction flooded my spirit and tears filled my eyes.

"Sorrow came, emptied your home." Yes! My HOME, and it still aches, Lord.

"Impulse to give up" and "sit in despair." Guilty. I am so weary from heartache.

"Line of battle" and "crisis at hand." I have fought as hard as I know how, God.

"To falter would imperil some holy interest." He has entrusted me with holy interests?

"Other lives harmed by my pausing." I feel so insignificant. What influence do I have?

"Should your hands be folded." Idleness. Father, I am WORN out by struggle.

"Do not linger even to indulge my grief." Help me, Lord, because this REALLY hurts!

Quiet tears turned to wracking sobs. I sat in my van for quite a while. Conviction and truth rang deep. There was no doubt in my mind. God had sovereignly planned this very moment just for me.

Just. For. Me.

On days of doubt and despair, I often come back to that devotional, not only to rally over the meaning of the message but to remember the powerful tenderness of God specifically lavished on me that day. And He can for you too. So hold on to the small moments when He speaks, for those moments produce great gains in your rebuilding. With that, please head to our final personal rebuilding time.

Personal Rebuilding

Look back at your original rubble heap. We started with words like *ransacked*, *destroyed*, *ruins*, and *exile*. Knowing there is nothing perfect and immediate about this process, describe what it looks like now. Even if the change is not in your circumstances but is a mind-set or heart change.

_____

_____

_____

_____

_____

What has been the biggest obstacle along the way? Or what still remains so? Even if it seems unchanged, please still bring it to the Lord now in prayer.

_____

_____

_____

_____

_____

The Israelites grew weary and needed to ask for the physical strength to continue. What has been the most wearisome to you? How are you seeking God's help to continue?

_____

_____

_____

_____

Here is a really hard question. If rebuilding has not progressed as quickly as you had hoped, how can you seek God and the support of others to persevere even still?

_____

_____

_____

_____

_____

How are you doing with not returning to the rubble you cleared away from your rebuilding?

_____

_____

_____

_____

_____

What blessings have you seen by resurrecting foundational stones?

_____

_____

_____

_____

_____

Do not miss this this step, dear one! For your LAST assignment, go back to the letter you wrote in the last lesson's Personal Rebuilding section on page 70. Read it out loud to yourself, and when you are ready, sign it. Consider sharing it with someone you trust. I am with you in spirit! Take a moment to do that now or make plans to do that with a friend, then come back to the final pages to wrap up.

Well done, friend! You have seen it through to the end, and that is no small feat! Oh, how I wish we could sit down over coffee and I could hear every detail of your journey through this book. I long to know HOW God spoke to you. I wonder WHAT the particular details of your rebuilding have been and WHERE in your life He is bringing beauty from ashes. But while I may never know the specifics of your story, I know God can bring restoration for you, just as He has for me and countless others.

So take the tools we have gleaned from Nehemiah and continue to apply them because there is still a battle ahead to fight. In the final image below, write any areas growth and victory you have seen so far.

BEAUTY FROM ASHES

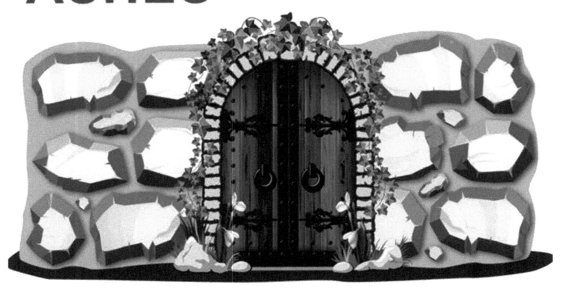

So what are my final thoughts? I will end with the exact verse that introduced me to Nehemiah eight years ago; only this time with the knowledge and respect the text deserves. Please read the next verse with passion in your soul.

"Don't be afraid of them. Remember the Lord, who is great and awesome, and fight for your brothers, your sons and your daughters, your wives and your homes" (Nehemiah 4:14b).

Remember all He has done. He will fight for you. And He is able to bring beauty from ashes.

"To bestow on them a crown of beauty instead of ashes" (Isaiah 61:3).

Please listen to your final worship song for this study. May it wash blessing upon blessing over you!

 "Beautiful Things" by Gungor

Thank you, dear one, for the pleasure of sharing the long journey through Nehemiah with you. If it would encourage you to share with me your story through this study, please e-mail me at beautyfromashesbook@gmail.com.